RECONNECTED
~to my bellybutton

RECONNECTED
~to my bellybutton

~ ~ ~

the rollercoaster journey of an
adoptee searching for family and roots

by **JOY BUDENSIEK**
Adoptee

Some names, places and dates have intentionally been
scrambled to protect individual privacy.
Amazingly, I found that both my birth and adoptive mother
have the same first name. For this book I again have given them
the same name—the universally beloved name Mary.

ISBN 0-9618730-9-4

PRINTED IN THE UNITED STATES OF AMERICA
1st Printing by Country Pines, Shoals, IN
2nd Printing by Maury Boyd & Assoc., Indianapolis, IN
(for printing information,
contact Mike McCoy: 888-897-9693)

RECONNECTED
~ to my bellybutton

The title caught your eye, didn't it?

That's what I wanted. I'm not trying to be rude or crude or offensive. Those who know me will tell you that's not my way. But for months, I contemplated and composed. Nothing fit.

Then in January 2001, through yet another incredible set of circumstances, I found myself seated at the table for Sunday dinner in the home of a Newfoundland family. I had met these kind people only thirty minutes before, at the close of church, when they had invited my daughter, granddaughter, and me home with them. Their Russian friends of about six years were invited also.

During dinner, the Russian lady turned to me and asked, "What are you doing up here?"

"I'm trying to do a little family history," I replied. "I was born in St. John's, then adopted by an American family. I'm trying to find out more about my birth family and the circumstances which led to my relinquishment and adoption."

For a moment she appeared puzzled, then with a look of clear understanding, she exclaimed, "Oh, in Russia, we say you are looking for your bellybutton!"

Now I was puzzled, but as the meaning of what she had just said registered, it made sense. "Yes," I agreed, "that's exactly what I'm doing."

Face it, everyone has a bellybutton! No one talks much about it—it's always been there. But, in its own way, it does remind us of our link to the past. No one (except Adam and Eve) arrived without a link to someone. Most people don't have far to look to see their link

~Dad and Mom aren't far away
~for me, I had to go looking to reconnect with mine.

DEDICATION

This book is lovingly dedicated

To my parents—both birth and adopted.
You gave me wonderful "roots"!

To John, my "forever love" and sharer
of dreams,
You have made life's road a journey
worth taking.

To the "leaves" — Julie, John Jr. Jim,
Bart, Ada
including our little "buds," Katie and Janie.

TO MY FRIENDS "ALONG THE WAY"

What an experience! For most authors, I suppose writing a book is mere routine, but for a first-timer like myself, it borders on stupidity. My brain does not define subject nominatives or indirect objects, much less their proper usage. I've been thankful for spell check, but it certainly isn't foolproof. But because of an incredible support group of friends and family, it's actually been fun; and I'm eager to see how God chooses to use the book in His kingdom. As Queen Esther came into the kingdom for "such a time as this," I was amazed again and again at how God brought people across my path for just such a time.

Linda Kelley, you were a God-send. You were teaching a class in journalism for Hobe Sound Bible College at the precise time I needed your expertise. Thank you for compiling my scraps of paper and combining them with hours of transcript for the first draft. Without you, who knows when it would have gotten off the ground.

Thank you, Dr. Ralph Woodworth and Dr. Ignacio Palacios, for wading through my very rough draft. Your professional opinions that "yes, this is a story worth publishing," were my encouragement to continue with the project.

9

Cousin Paul Ehr, Joe and Gay Taylor, Imelda Mabus, and Lynn Wilson—my unofficial advisory committee—sacrificed several hours to help make the story "reader friendly." My appreciation is extended to each of you.

The words of wisdom and sensitivity from Richard and Carol Curtis and Carole Greene, my friends from the Martin County Adoption Support Group helped me so much. Let's face it, people involved in the adoption triad do have different perspectives. Thanks—you cannot know how much I valued your input.

Ann Coates, what can I say? You were there before the first word was put on paper. Your suggestions, encouragement, and candid advice steered me in the right direction, and I'm grateful.

Thank you, Dr. Wayne Hopkins, and Sherrie Eldridge for lending your endorsements on the back cover. Because I have always had the deepest respect for you, I consider myself doubly blessed to have received your support.

Wes Peterson—we've learned together, haven't we? What a challenge you had to take my mental pictures and put it on paper. I like it! And, Rob Scott, your skill has given the cover the professional touch of class it needed. I deeply appreciate the expertise of you both.

My special recognition is given to Anna Mae Ehr, my adoptive mother's sister, who, in the absence of my mother, walked through this experience with me. Your selfless and giving spirit has always shone brightly, and I especially appreciated it when we talked so candidly about my early family life. You could have insisted that I "sugar-coat" some sensitive family matters, but instead you have allowed the story to be told, hoping perhaps it will help others.

Betty Predmore—for some time, we've talked and dreamed of holding this published story in our hands. It's actually happened! You truly do have a "gift" of composition and editing. You have breathed life into the story and made it a page-turner. I was confident the story was safe with you. Thank you for the many hours of labor. And, Tara Hydes, thank you for being your mother's transcriber and typist. You stepped into the gap to make it happen, and I deeply appreciate the hours you have given.

Country Pines—for months I could not decide if I should locate a publisher or self-publish. Your expertise, guidance and knowledge of printing have made me very happy to be a self-publisher, and I'm proud of the product you've given me.

Julie and John, Jr., having your own families spared you from having to sit at the supper table night after night to hear all the chatter. But your interest and support for your mother's "pet project" came through in many ways. Thank you both.

John, Sr. and Jim—it's finished! It was you who sat through the day by day unfolding of my dream and all the challenges it entailed. Our own inside jokes relating to this project helped lighten the load. Thank you, Hon, for standing by my side once again. It has been a gigantic mountain to climb, and you have pulled me up and over time and time again. And dear Jim—my fellow dreamer—it's been fun as I've worked on my book, and you've taken your first steps into aerial photography. The projects, of course, do not resemble each other, but our dreaming, scheming, monologues, and one-track minds are strangely similar. Our supper times were truly a three-ring circus of shared new horizons.

And, last but not least, to my many dear friends who felt like running when they saw me approaching with a handful of papers, I say thanks from the bottom of my heart. Special thanks to Mrs. Alberta Lone, to whom I had to give an account of the "book progress" every day before getting my dinner! This really did happen before you turned 100! Tonya Bailey and Jenness Peak, you were a daily source of smiles and kind notes, which helped me keep focused. I cannot begin to name everyone who has played a part to help *RECONNECTED to my bellybutton* become a realty, but your encouragement has been invaluable to me.

Heavenly Father, it is You to Whom I owe my deepest appreciation and praise. When I reflect upon the timetable and events of my life, I stand in awe of Your love and mercy. As always, You gave me what I needed when I needed it. You knew that when my family "nest" began to empty, I would need a challenge to occupy my time and energy and give me a sense of purpose. Thank you for entrusting me with this unique "loaves and fishes" to offer in return to You.

PREFACE

Everyone has a story, and the little book you are about to read happens to be mine. Approximately 22 million members of the adoption triad are scattered all over the United States, and believe me, all 22 million of us have a tale to tell. Merely saying the word "adoption" evokes strong emotions.

For some, adoption has been the life through whom their family circle has been made complete. For others, adoption has been the intruder that has stolen not only their flesh and blood but also their heart and mind in a lifetime of pain and memory. The stories of adoptions are as varied as the snowflakes. I've read enough books, talked to enough people, and sat through the long periods of silence where the emotions were too deep for words to realize that while there are many common threads each of us has his or her own solitary drama.

And yet for this to be "my story," I would have had to be the planner, the one who made it happen—obviously, I wasn't. Babies don't make decisions. And babies don't determine where and when, or to whom and under what circumstances, they are born. God does. His plan began long before I reached planet earth. My life is simply a continuation of the miraculous intervention of God in the human affairs of His creation.

From my earliest memory, I have known three things about my adoption. First, **I was adopted**. No one ever tried to hide that fact from me. Secondly, **I was loved**. Never for one second did I ever question that love. And, thirdly, **I would find out who I was**—someday, somehow, somewhere.

I keenly remember the shock of being asked, "Why did you search for your birth parents?" *Why?* Well, I just never thought about the "why." Always, the question was "*when*?" To search for my roots was as much a part of living as graduation, getting married, raising a family—it was something that *had* to happen. My motivations were not pain, rejection, or the gaping hole of loss that so many experience. It was simply that I could not imagine going to my grave and never trying to find who I was. I *had* to find the genetic "drummer" who beat the rhythm to which I marched.

Today, I know the answers to many of the questions that I initially had. But for many years the pieces just didn't fit. God did finally put together some of the puzzle pieces of my life, but He is choosing to fit them together only a piece at a time. Life is lived in sequence, and this book will take you on the same journey through time that I took. As human beings, we would like to see the end from the beginning, but in retrospect, I can truly say God's timing is perfect. Receiving the puzzle pieces one at a time allowed me to mentally and emotionally digest, enjoy and appreciate even the smallest detail. And so, my friend, you too will live the story in chronological order—just as I have!

My purpose in writing this book is not to solve all the problems of the adoption triad—there is an incredible wealth of excellent material on the subject already printed. It is not to provide simplistic answers to those who have been emotionally wounded, nor is it merely the chatter of a "happy ending" story. My purpose, rather, is to share with the readers the incredible roller-coaster ride of a child answering the primal call to unravel the mystery of her life and show the infinite care of a heavenly Father Whose eyes have not escaped even the smallest detail.

If, when you lay this book down, your reaction is, "Wow, God really does love, He does care, He truly does have a design to my life!" then these words will not be just another story.

1

"YOU'RE DOING WHAT?"

And now abideth faith, hope, charity, these three;
But the greatest of these is charity
(I Corinthians 13:13).

"You're doing what? Let me get this straight. You're telling me that you left West Palm Beach, Florida, this morning, and are flying to St. John's, Newfoundland, this evening to look for a woman whose name you don't even know?" queried the distinguished-looking man across the aisle from me.

"Yes, sir, I am. I know it sounds crazy. But you must remember, she isn't just any woman—she's my mother. I'm adopted. When I was only three months old, I was given up for adoption. I've always known I was adopted and that someday I would go back to discover who I am. I guess that day has come."

Here I was flying somewhere between Quebec and Halifax, 33,000 feet in the air, talking to a gentleman who I was to learn later was a retired airline pilot. Obviously, he was skeptical, but congenial nevertheless.

After a few more bites of dinner, he resumed our conversation. "To be honest with you, it's not unusual to see people up here in the North Country searching for their roots or genealogy or, like yourself, their birth parents. I understand that there were about 3,000 Newfie babies taken to the States after their adopted parents' tour of duty ended. I guess the part that blows my mind is that you have nothing to go on, nothing definite."

"No, I really don't. I don't know her name. I don't know where she lives. I don't know if she married or has another family. I *am* fairly certain that she's alive, at least she was two months ago when the social services let her know I was searching for her."

Shaking his head and trying hard to understand my predicament, he asked the logical question, "Why didn't you just go through the social services and let them make the connection?"

"I did; believe me, I tried. In fact, I've waited *six years* for my particular case to surface to the top of the 'caseload pile.' And the social services were great, but in order for them to complete the search and bring everything full circle, my birth mother had to consent to meet me. She was found and told of my wishes, but for whatever reasons, her response in essence was: 'Thanks for telling me my baby is okay, but no thanks, I'm not interested in going any further.'"

"Ouch, that hurt, didn't it?"

"Yes—yes, it did. I don't know why I was given up the first time, but then to be told a second time, 'thanks, but no thanks.' Yes, it hurt, incredibly." This stranger could not possibly understand just how painful those memories were.

"Well, if you were given up once and rejected again as recently as two months ago, why in the world are you on this plane, headed for only God knows what?" His mood had shifted from sympathy to compassionate disbelief.

"That's a good question, except that I believe in God. You wouldn't believe all the circumstances that have seemed to point me in the direction of actually going there to try to make some sense of all this. Sir, do you believe in miracles?" My own mood had changed from the recent painful memories to the mission of hope at hand.

Chuckling, he leaned back, never really giving me an answer. But I could tell he was skeptical of the idea of a God, especially one who would send one of His children on such a wild-goose chase!

"Well, I believe! Let me tell you just one of those circumstances. Today is Tuesday. Sunday at church, I was telling a friend of mine that in two days I planned to fly to St. John's, Newfoundland, to try to find my mom. He said that he was working at a private beach on Jupiter Island (north of West Palm Beach) when he noticed a wine bottle washed up on the sand. A half-covered bottle always carries an air of mystery so he picked it up. Sure enough, a piece of paper was inside, which he saved. The name and address on that paper was people from St. John's, Newfoundland. We both were flabbergasted at the 'coincidences' involved. Sir, I have that name and address right here in my bag. Now, would you call that a miracle or would you call that a miracle?" I couldn't help but smile. Things like that just don't happen in real life. But this truly had happened. It was like living a mystery.

"What are you going to do with it? Do you know the people?"

"No, I don't. I don't know *anybody* on that island, and I'm not sure how the whole thing is going to fit together, but one thing I *know*—this didn't happen by chance!"

Shaking his head, he grudgingly conceded, "Yes, maybe you *should* be on this plane. Maybe it isn't such a wild-goose chase, after all. Tell you what, here is my name and address. Keep me posted."

Tucking his scrap of paper into my bag, I again smiled. God was planning to do something special and even this newfound friend, skeptical and perhaps a little hard-hearted, didn't want to be left out. True, I didn't have a clue as to how things would turn out, but I was confident that the God Who had begun a good work had something exciting in store. Little did I know the crooked path about to unfold.

Meanwhile, our little plane continued to skim through the North Atlantic skies as we each munched on our peanuts. He sipped his Vodka; I sipped my Coke, each of us lost in our own private reverie.

The plane landed, the door opened, and I stepped out onto the crunchy snow. It was February 1, 1997.

I made my way into the airport at Halifax, Nova Scotia, one island away from being "home." True, that one island represented a distance of 1500 ground miles but this was the closest I'd been to the place of my birth. Scanning the faces of the weary travelers scattered on the terminal benches awaiting their next flight, I wondered. *Do they look like me? Is that guy sitting over in the corner my half-brother? Hmm, that whole family over there has high foreheads, just like mine.* I look; I wonder. Chances are that no one in this waiting area actually shares my blood. But, then again, who's to say they don't? That's the joy, the fascination, the apprehension and the mystery of being adopted. *We do not know.* But enough reverie—back to the business at hand.

One by one, we shuffle past the reservation desk, into the waiting area. Life here is certainly different from that in Florida—I can feel it in the air. There's a relaxed pace. The language is English but with pronounced inflections of French and British-Canadian. I have to listen carefully.

"Ladies and gentleman, all passengers leaving Halifax on non-stop flight 1488 for St. John's,

Newfoundland, be advised that the plane will be departing at 9:10 p.m." Glancing at my watch, I realize I have thirty minutes before I need to be back. Half an hour to go down memory's lane. *Somewhere in this terminal there's a front door,* I thought, *with steps leading up to that door. I want to go back to that spot.*

It was at that spot six years earlier when God changed the intentions of my husband and myself from flying to St. John's; therefore, we had time to leisurely enjoy and explore the beauties of Nova Scotia. When we stood in this place six years ago, we did not know the miracles God would bring about from that clear sense of direction. But for tonight, I just wanted to go back and express my appreciation to my heavenly Father. *Thank you, God. Your thoughts are truly so much more infinitely wise. Your plans are so much higher and wiser than ours. Thank you for being my heavenly Shepherd and leading me every step of the way.*

"Ladies and gentlemen, all passengers going from Halifax to St. John's on flight 1488 may now board at Gate 4. Please have your boarding pass available."

St. John's! *Saint John's*, Newfoundland! Just to see that name spelled out in big bold print sent shivers through my body. I had dreamed about this place for so long and now to *actually* be standing in a line headed to St. John's! **Wow**! After years of dreaming, fantasizing, hoping, and one hundred other emotions, these words symbolized the beginning of a dream. Hopefully, this would not be a nightmare come true.

~ ~ ~

As our little plane lifted into the inky sky, the lights of Nova Scotia became dimmer and sparser, finally fading all together. Somewhere, we left the shores of Nova Scotia, crossed part of the Atlantic Ocean, and entered the province of Newfoundland. Nobody sat close to me on this leg of the journey, but that was okay. God and I had a lot of talking to do. And yet it wasn't really talking. I had come to a point when only my heart could speak. My thoughts were too jumbled, my emotions too high and too raw to put into words.

How do I describe returning to the land of my birth? How do I describe knowing that in the little villages thousands of feet below are people whose blood carries the same genes as mine? How can I possibly express the anxiety of perhaps being told for the third time, "Thanks but no thanks, you live your life, and I'll live mine?" How do I describe the persistent longing to know my roots? How do I convey the deep conviction that I am living a drama, not written by myself, but by the beautiful hand of a loving heavenly Father? Somewhere deep inside I recognize this isn't my story alone, but a message to be lived and shared, a testimony to the order, design, care, and guidance of the God Who created the stars so radiantly shining outside the plane window?

The hour and thirty-minute flight went by very quickly. The plane, which had followed the coastline, now turned north, beginning its descent, and the lights of the Avalon Peninsula began to come into clear focus.

"Ladies and gentlemen, we are beginning our final descent into the St. John's International Airport, St. John's, Newfoundland. The flight attendant will be around to pick up any last minute items. Please make sure your seat belts are buckled securely. This is our final destination."

I had come home. In one sense, this was a final destination but, in another, only the beginning.

2

THE ADOPTION OPTION

"All the world's a stage,
And all the men and women merely players:
They have their exits and their entrances
And one man in his time plays many parts"
(William Shakespeare).

Lives are lived against the backdrop of the big picture, and events half way around the world have a way of impacting lives. In the early morning hours of December 7, 1941, the American people awakened to screaming headlines splashed all across their newspapers:

"UNITED STATES ENTERS W.W. II"
"UNITED STATES OFFICIALLY DECLARES
WAR ON GERMANY"
"THE UNITED STATES JOINS THE ALLIES"

Our country was drawn into war, and now the individual lives of American men and women everywhere were changed. Men were drafted, and women went to work outside the home to run the industrial world—all for the cause of freedom.

Plans for the future were either moved forward or placed on hold. No longer was life normal.

~ ~ ~

Two years earlier the British had declared war against Germany, placing the Canadian military at war also. Canadian military forces had joined with the British forces and now served under the Royal Armed Forces, fighting side by side with their mother country. It would be another nine years before Newfoundland actively elected to become part of Canada, but in heart, soul and strength, a disproportionately large number of Newfound-landers volunteered for active duty under the Canadian flag.

The American military recognized the strategic location of Newfoundland. It needed military bases stationed as close to the North Atlantic War Theater as possible, and Newfoundland was the logical choice. During the early hours on January 29, 1941, the U.S.A.T. *Edmund B. Alexander* steamed through the Narrows, quickly followed by hundreds more battle-ready ships. In a little over two years, the Americans had "moved in," establishing 77 military installations in Newfoundland and Labrador, where over 100,000 Americans would eventually be stationed. Some bases were small, with only a few men manning important outposts and deciphering the enemy codes; other bases were large, bustling with activity and importance.

Gander was the world's busiest airport, with 250 planes taking off and landing during a typical day. Many men left the shores of Newfoundland in bombing raids, never to return.

But many *did* return, and there never seemed to be a dull moment in Newfoundland. The atmosphere was not one of war, but more of a party. Newfoundland would never be the same.

Imagine a small remote country where life had always revolved around fishing suddenly being inundated with American soldiers. The average age of these men was 21, and for most it was the first time to be away from home. The Newfoundlanders rolled out the red carpet of welcome and worked alongside these young allies in civilian jobs to create such military installations as Fort Pepperall, Argentia Naval Base, Harmon Air Force Base, and other smaller bases. The Newfoundlanders remember those days as a special time in their history—never before (or since) had there been so much excitement crackling in the air. At no other time had *every* season of the year seen so much activity, so much life. Plenty of entertainment abounded, with gals and guys available with just a mere turn of the head. Yes, it *was* a grand time. In fact, the Newfoundlanders themselves call it "The Friendly Invasion."

The war ended. It was still in the 1940s. Many soldiers went home, although not all the military bases shut down. The Americans were there to stay for awhile.

Against this backdrop, the '50s came and my story continues. Some of the people involved in the unfolding drama had been there for centuries, while circumstances brought others. Thus it was with Jack and Mary, my adoptive parents.

Edward "Jack" Comadoll was orphaned at age seven, to be raised by a stern step-aunt. His mother had died giving birth to his younger brother. It was kind of his aunt to take her brother's children to raise after he was killed in a train-car accident, yet

Early days in Brownsville

for some reason, it seemed to Jack that she always favored the other children and life became unbearable for him. The military appeared to be a good way out of a bad situation and at age fifteen, he left home to follow Uncle Sam. That road led from Ohio to California, Mississippi, Hawaii, and to Christmas Island during WWI. During a leave on which he went to visit his brother in Pennsylvania, he met Mary Taylor, a railroader's daughter from Appalachian USA. It was nearly love at first sight, and the next leave found Jack returning to Pennsylvania to tie the knot with Mary.

Life wasn't always easy, but it certainly held variety at every turn. Jack's military term of enlistment came to an end with an honorable discharge, and he returned to civilian life—but never for long. After so many years in the military, civilian life didn't seem to "fit" and off he would go to enlist for another tour of duty. The Marines, Army, Air Force—Jack joined them all.

The early 1950s found the Comadolls stationed at Eglin Air Force Base, Florida, awaiting their next orders.

"Well, Mary, the military has gone and done it again."

"Jack, didn't you ask to be assigned somewhere in the Pittsburgh area? These orders don't look like Pittsburgh to me. Ernest Harmon Air Force Base, Stephenville, Newfoundland. Newfoundland? Where's *that*?"

So out comes the map, or rather the atlas, and there, perched on the extreme eastern coast of North America, is a relatively large island called Newfoundland. A quick trip to the encyclopedia tells them about the jagged, sea-smashed coastline, the giant fishing industry which fuels the economy, and the helter-skelter villages which dot the 10,000 miles of coastline. The insular location and internal isolation of small communities produce unique cultural characteristics. The Irish influence creates a living archive of folk music, storytelling, and folklore.

What the encyclopedia did not tell the Comadolls was that the island was inhabited by some of the most warmhearted, lovable, indomitable, spirited people to be found anywhere. Nearly everyone who has visited the island agrees that its most valued resource is the spirit of its people. The books also fail to mention that entering Newfoundland is like stepping back in time. The people have an easy-going pace to life that adds an important dimension to reality. Human respect and individual dignity is simply the expected way of life. Until recently, the St. John's city policemen did not even carry guns. The need didn't exist.

In my growing up years, Mom loved to recall the whiteout snowstorms. I remember being told that in the more remote parts of the island, moose roamed freely and if the mood struck, a mama moose would feed her calf in the middle of the road. Other memorable experiences of their life in this enchanting northern fairyland made wonderful bedtime stories.

Yes, Newfoundland in the '50s was a neat place to be, and this is where Jack's military orders assigned him. From the best they could determine, married housing on the base was hard to come by, so in anticipation of their needs, a 30-foot Spartan house trailer was purchased. Leaving Pittsburgh, Pennsylvania, the trailer was shipped by rail, later put on a ferry, and was finally parked at Russell's Trailer Park in Stephenville, Newfoundland.

Jack and Mary were happy. He faithfully served his country through two World Wars, and now he was reaching the end of what would eventually be a nearly forty-year military career. Now that he's older, an assignment as chaplain's assistant suited him fine. Mary, laid back and quiet, let life come as it might, and for the most part, was happy to watch the snow fall, with one exception—for years they had wanted children. None came. They didn't talk about it, even to their family; in those days you just didn't talk about things like that. But their dreams, their hopes, their unanswered prayers of many years were never forgotten. Jack and Mary didn't know that their steps had led them to the one place in all the world where adoptions were probably easier to come by than anywhere else at that time.

Adoption—something never really considered, but now—maybe, just maybe it was an option. New hope was born. It seemed they stood a good chance, with one potential problem—their ages. Mary was 35 years old; Jack, 50. So it was that sometime in May 1950, the first official inquiry was dropped into the mailbox. Paperwork, health examinations, more paperwork, references, and recommendations by the military were gathered, processed, and sent to the welfare office at Cornerbrook.

"Jack!" The usually quiet Mary is nearly beside herself with excitement as she bursts into the base chapel where Jack was sweeping. "Sorry for disturbing you at work, but I just had to get in touch with you. It came today! It came, it *really* did!"

"Now sit down, Mary, and talk to me calmly

Jack and Mary in Newfoundland just before I arrived

and intelligently. What came? What's so important that you came all the way over here in this awful weather?"

"A letter from the social services. They got our application. Listen! It says he 'will contact the agencies concerned and make a decision regarding the placement of a child with you for adoption.'"

With trembling hands, Mary continues reading, "Oh, listen, it also says, 'When we hear anything further concerning your application, we will notify you immediately. Yours truly, C. J. Spurrell, Regional Welfare Supervisor.' Jack! Do you understand what this means? It means they are actually processing our papers. It means that we can actually begin to dream!"

Now the wait was on.

At times, there were long stretches with no communication from the welfare office. During one of those interminable stretches, Jack and Mary were encouraged. Even though they had heard nothing directly from the local offices, they knew the system was working behind the scenes. Evidently the Newfoundland agents had contacted the social services in the Uniontown, Pennsylvania, area to check on their character and ability to take on this parental responsibility. A social worker actually visited Mary's family and must have been favorably impressed, because the adoption process continued to inch forward.

3

A "GIRL-CHILD IS BORN"

*To every thing there is a season, and a time
to every purpose under the heaven:
A time to be born
(Ecclesiastes 3:1,2).*

Long before I was even thought of, God had another important stage of my life already set in place.

William and Catherine Booth could not possibly have seen how far and wide the loving arms of their ministry would reach. What originally began on London's east end quickly spread across the Atlantic and reached Canada in 1882. Shortly thereafter, a little lady by the name of Emma Churchill Dawson felt led to reach out to the masses of St. John's. Emma was the eleventh officer commissioned in the new Canadian territory. Salvation Army policy stated that if a commissioned officer married "out of rank," they must temporarily resign. It was during this "furlough" that Emma and Charles came to Newfoundland to wait out

their six-months' leave of absence. They considered
it their honeymoon.

But they could not keep the Good News of salvation quiet. Commissioned or non-commissioned
made no difference to them. The Dawsons
announced services to be held in Portugal Cove and
St. John's. In retrospect, the Salvation Army
arrived in Newfoundland as a form of spontaneous
combustion. Stories abound of those early days
when the corps members would march through the
streets, taking inquisitive bystanders along with
them, until they reached the Army temple where
an emotional and demonstrative evangelistic service was held.

The Army made its mark. Thousands were not
only converted, but received the love and care of
people who put their religion into action. Salvation,
along with social action, became their trademark.
No matter what unfortunate social fallout came as
a result of sin, the Army was there to lend a helping hand in the Name of Jesus. They not only
talked the talk of their beliefs, they walked the
walk with their lives. Bramwell Booth once said,
"We carry our theology in a knapsack because we
are always on the move." They lived their religion
in a beautiful practical way. And they made a difference.

The original Army congregation in St. John's
grew. Visions for new works across town sprang up.
What we would call "rehab" centers today were

established. Drunkards, gamblers, prostitutes—you name it—sin had not taken them so low that they couldn't find forgiveness, healing, and a new life in Christ. The Salvation Army people were sensitive to whatever social needs surrounded them, and the innocent unfortunates of society were embraced also. If an occasion of need arose, they arose to the occasion.

One of the Army's challenges was the large number of girls who found themselves "in the family way." Abortion wasn't an option; it was considered sin, and it was also illegal. Some girls went to "visit an aunt," but if that opportunity didn't exist, what was a girl to do? The Salvation Army was there to help meet the need by providing homes for unwed mothers.

What began downtown on Cook Street as the "Anchorage," referred to as a "receiving home," later moved to a newly donated building on Torbay Road. Sometime in 1949 the name transitioned to Glenbrook Home for Unwed Mothers. This home remained in operation from 1949 to 1965 when it ceased to exist. But the year of my story is 1951 and the Home was in full operation on one cold, snowy night.

~ ~ ~

Typically, Newfoundland nights are cold and it was cold again this night, with temperatures tumbling into the 20s. A new snow had fallen and nobody wanted to venture out into the night. It was a night when one wants to sit by the fireplace, munch popcorn, dream dreams, or read the latest novel. An air of peace, bittersweet peace, permeated the air at Glenbrook Home for Unwed Mothers.

Nearly all the rooms were full. There were girls in their eighth and ninth months of pregnancy. Some mothers had delivered only a day or two ago. There were mothers and newborns waiting—waiting for the right couple to come along who wanted to adopt a baby.

Each mother had two things in common. Life would be so much simpler if the choices that brought them to this home in the first place had never been made. And secondly, each girl knew she was loved and cared for with respect and dignity, regardless of the circumstances. Her baby was loved too; this wasn't one of those baby-selling

Formerly Glenbrook Home for Unwed Mothers

houses. These people weren't in this business for the money. The dedicated workers were there because they loved, and their love was put into action.

Nurse Winnie Reed looked out the window. It was late, very late. When that last city bus passed by the Home, she would check on her young charges, turn off the light, and call it a day. But wait, what's this?

The bus stopped, and a young girl disembarked. She was heavy, very heavy, with child. She caught her breath as the cold air hit her full in the face, and she felt those awful cramps in her lower back. She struggled to find the path. Never before had she been in this predicament, but from somewhere deep within her female psyche, she instinctively knew it wouldn't be long until her baby arrived. *Thank God, the porch light is still on and the reflection on the snow gives me light to see the road.* This was a night she would never forget.

Drawing her warm nurse's cape around her shoulders, Nurse Reed opened the door and stepped out into the swirling snow, hurrying to the shadowy figure coming closer. The wind howled and blew the snow, swirling it around the two figures as they come closer to each other. They reached each other, one with outstretched arms, the other only too willing to fall into those comforting arms.

Throughout the night, the labor pains tore through her body with intensity. There wasn't the comfort of a husband or even family nearby. This was a solitary journey. Motherhood was thrust upon a young girl who was only a child herself. Sometime in the wee hours of the morning a "girl child" was born. She was rather small, just a bit over five pounds, with dark hair and slanted eyes. If one didn't know better, you would have thought she had a touch of Oriental blood in her.

Mission complete. Under the watchful eye of their nurse, mother and child nestled together in safety and care. It had been a long, long night. Now it was time to sleep, to forget about the past and the future. Time was held suspended—mother and daughter together enveloped in love.

However, that suspended time only lasted a few hours. Decisions had to be made; futures had to be planned and considered. What was best for the mother? for the child? What were the options?

Since the beginning of this ordeal, the word "adoption" kept creeping into the picture. It seemed the only way out. To never see her baby again, to relinquish her to an unknown world seemed unthinkable, but what else could she do? No one pushed her, yet week after week the social services people visited the Home, reassuring each mother that there were indeed people—lots of people—who were willing and quite capable of helping her in this situation. They would love her child, and do their best to raise her baby.

When this new mother looked into the trusting face of her little girl, the feelings of guilt and deser-tion were overwhelming. But the reality of her circumstance forced her into making yet another painful decision—adoption was her only choice.

"Bring the adoption relinquishment papers to me. I have decided to sign."

Once the decision was made, the "waiting game" began. The social services once again had to verify their information. Arrangements had to be made for the adoptive parents to be in town. Legal work had to be notarized. Sometimes it seemed so cold and calculated, but for the mother and her baby, the emotional heartstrings were stronger than ever.

~ ~ ~

The Salvation Army did an admirable job of providing for the physical needs of its "charges," but the concerns went further than that. They prayed for each baby and mother. On one of those precious "identifying information" papers, which I received decades later, I discovered that I was dedicated to God on February 3, 1952. I don't know, of course, if it was a service dedicating several children or one specifically for me, but I can visualize the faithful Salvation Army worker taking me in her arms and offering a prayer similar to this:

"Lord, today we bring this little one to you. We don't know what her future holds, but You do. Dear heavenly Father, be with her, guide her, direct her, watch over her. And if it be Your will someday,

Lord, will You use her in Your kingdom? Lord, bless this dear mother today. You know the pain she is going through. Will You wrap Your arms of love around her? Be close to her. Don't let the mistakes of the past take away her future. Help this mother and child to someday be reunited around Your throne in the sweet bye-and-bye. We ask this in Jesus' Name. Amen."

~ ~ ~

Eyes misty with emotion, Miss Barstook gently kissed the precious little baby whom she had just dedicated before placing her back in her mother's arms, arms that would soon be empty. But no one could stop the prayers or the hand of God at work regardless of the many miles, days, or even years that would separate this mother and child.

Then it was time. The dreaded day arrived. Watching from the upstairs window, Mary peered out as the social worker parked her car and walked toward the building. She knew that when the social worker left the building that day, she would carry in her arms Mary's most precious gift of life—and her life would never, ever be the same. Somewhere locked away in the subconscious memories of the mind, where nature mercifully removes those scenes too painful to remember, there would be the memory of that last kiss, the last hug, and the last baby scent. The emotional walls of protection would continue to build.

4

"I DON'T CARE ABOUT THE DIAPER RASH"

God setteth the solitary in families
(Psalms 68:6).

On the other side of the Island, meanwhile, the Newfoundland winter had gotten long. Snow, which had been so pretty, had long since lost its charm. The skies were dreary and overcast most of the time and, worst of all, the spirits of Jack and Mary matched the world around them. Weeks had gone by without a word from social services, and they found that silence wasn't always golden. Sometimes it was nerve-wracking, depressing, and discouraging. But long, emotional nights do end—this one ended with the ring of the telephone.

"Mr. Comadoll. This is Mr. Spurrell from the welfare office. We are calling to confirm that you and your wife, Mary, are still interested in adopting. Is that correct?"

"Yes, sir, it is," Jack stammered into the phone, while wildly waving his arms for Mary to come closer to listen.

"Mr. Comadoll, it is important for me to confirm this because a baby girl was born in the eastern part of the province in December. As things look now, she may be available for adoption the end of February. We'll keep in touch."

The stunned parents-to-be sat down and, through their tears of happiness, considered the news that they were indeed about to be parents, exactly nine months after the process began! A call was quickly placed to Brownsville, Pennsylvania, where an anxiously awaiting extended family received the news that Jack and Mary's "special blessing" was born in December.

~ ~ ~

February 26, 1951—the court-appointed day to become parents. Not exactly the way most people have babies—no labor pains, no harrowing ride to the hospital, no frantic calls to family and friends, but an incredibly emotional day just the same.

Records show that the Newfoundland adoption placement social services of the '40s and '50s was a well-oiled, efficient agency. This is not meant to be a derogatory description. Given the large number of girls who wished (or were forced) to give their babies for adoption, this office operated with compassion and sensitivity.

Mary Comadoll was not the only woman from Harmon Air Force Base finding her way to the plane that morning. A newfound friend, Lois Todd, was also going to receive her baby boy. Quick kisses, a few anxious tears, and one last embrace left the two "soon-to-be-fathers" on the tarmac, as their wives boarded the plane which would take them across the island to St. John's and their new future.

I can only guess what must have gone through my mother's mind as she boarded the plane taking her from Cornerbrook (on the western side of the island) to St. John's (the eastern-most point on the North American continent). There were probably moments of intense chatter, but most likely, she was quiet and reflective. I'm quite sure she wasn't thinking of the geography, but rather of the new little one God was about to give them. A quick peek once again into the diaper bag must have reassured her that she was prepared as best as she knew. Diapers, pins, bottles and blankets—everything was there. More important and most treasured was a special dress sent from her family for this memorable occasion.

In retrospect, after visiting St. John's, I wish I had some answers: Where did my mom stay? How did she get around town? Did the streets of St. John's remind her of Brownsville, Pennsylvania? Did we stay in the same area? Were the buildings she entered the same ones I visited forty-four years later? Those details and many others are permanently buried, but one thing was certain, Mary was on her way to get her baby girl!

February 26, 1951—the day my parents coined as my "Happy Day." One more momentous decision had to be made.

"Mrs. Comadoll."

"Yes," replied Mary, timidly.

"You are here to adopt a baby girl, right?"

"Yes, ma'am."

"In our communication with you, we told you that the baby you will be getting was born December 30, but since then another baby girl, born in October, is available for adoption. Mrs. Comadoll, we strongly recommend that you adopt the baby born in October rather than the baby born in December."

Now, in my reflections on the past, I try to imagine my timid, easygoing mother being forced to make such a choice. She had not yet seen either of the babies, so she didn't have much to go on. One determining factor came to mind. She had already told her mother (my grandmother) that the baby they were going to adopt was born in December. So, based on this one small fact, my fate was decided—I would become their baby.

"Madam, I want the baby born in December."

"Are you sure, Mrs. Comadoll? Trust us. The baby born in October is much prettier and the last time we checked, the December baby has diaper rash."

But the decision was made; there would be no turning back. Diaper rash or no diaper rash, *I was her baby.*

~ ~ ~

Aside from the legal papers and formula instructions, my mother did not receive any "identifying information" papers. If she had, I'm sure I would have seen them at some time during my life. They simply did not exist. And Mom was too excited to ask many questions.

For many years, my only sense of roots and information about my birth parents were these small scraps of information: 1) my birth mother was from Newfoundland, 2) my birth father was in the United States Military, stationed in Newfoundland at the time of my conception, 3) my mother was of medium build, with dark hair, 4) she had a pleasing personality, and 5) my mother really cared about me. Importantly, she cared enough about me that she specifically asked that I be placed with a strongly religious, Protestant family. Of course, this didn't leave me with a lot of information, but it was all I had for many years. It was enough, and I was satisfied until I could begin to make some discoveries for myself.

I suppose many questions probably could have been asked by my adopted mother, but the idea simply never occurred to her. When she left the social services agency that day, most of the juicy tidbits of identity were left behind. At the end of that work day, the last human link between my birth mother and my adoptive mother would forever be locked behind the door, and with it, secrets would be forever locked from me.

~ ~ ~

With a sigh of relief and incredible excitement, Mary Comadoll completed all the formalities, the paperwork and signatures. And then they brought me to my mom. Barren arms of thirty-six years were

Proud new mother

filled with a beautiful little black-haired, ten-pound bundle who squirmed and wiggled and looked at her with those big slanted eyes. One word only could even begin to touch the emotions of that moment—*joy!*

Proud new father

Returning to the hotel, then later reboarding the plane, Mary flew the same air miles back home. Unlike Naomi of old, who went out full and came back empty, Mary went out empty and came back full.

Jack anxiously waited at the airport and upon arrival, the new little family of three joyfully headed to their home. A new chapter in the life of Jack and Mary Comadoll began.

Sandra Lynn, the name my birth mother gave me, now became Joylene Irene Comadoll. "Joy" symbolized the happiness brought into their lives; "lene" because my mom thought it was unique and different and she liked the sound of it; "Irene" after my maternal grandmother. Daddy and Mom were ecstatically happy; their world was now complete. But, never for one moment did they take this child for granted or the blessing she brought into their lives.

~ ~ ~

It would have been impossible for my adoptive mother to know that while she was in St. John's, only a few blocks away another mother, young and brokenhearted, had kissed her baby for the last time, squared her shoulders, and determined within herself to return to normal life. But exactly how would she do that when her heart was gone and her mother-arms empty?

5

RIGHT, SAFE AND HONORABLE

I pledge allegiance to the flag
Of the United States of America . . .
(American Pledge).

Parenting—a brand new skill that neither parent knew much about. Some things come naturally, however, and this was *their* baby girl, to have and to hold. If Dolly Mutt, their old cocker spaniel could have talked, she would have told of strange conversations in the middle of the night.

"Mary, I haven't heard any noises from the crib in the last ten minutes. Is she still breathing?"

For the umpteenth time that night, a flashlight was grabbed; and, yes, her little chest was still going up and down. Angels had not whisked away their little joy.

Bottles, formulas, and shots at the military base—every day revolved around the new little jewel in their lives.

The weather broke with the melting snow and spring came. Southern winds beckoned the family to explore the outdoors. Wrapped up and perched in a little red wagon, they went everywhere. Life was good.

There was just one small fly in the ointment. Sergeant Comadoll received orders that his next tour of military duty would begin at Pittsburgh, Pennsylvania, in June 1952. But for some unknown reason, the adoption process was stalled. Even though much of the paperwork had been completed at the time of adoption, it was not finalized. By the fine letter of the law, there was still a possibility that their little girl could be taken from them. What had happened? Why was there such a lack of communication from the social services? In the still hours of the night, an icy hand would clutch their hearts as they wondered what was stalling the final papers. Had the birth mother requested the return of her baby? Had their files been reviewed and the decision made that they were too old after all? Had a social worker been watching unknowingly? Until that final legal step was taken, there was always the heart-wrenching thought that this could end.

The Comadolls lived with this ever-nagging fear for over a year but, finally, on May 10, 1952, before the Magistrate W. H. W. Strong, the Clerk of Summary Jurisdiction at Cornerbrook, Newfoundland, the adoption was completed. Mary wrote in her daughter's baby book, " *Joylene Irene was lawfully adopted by Edward C. and Mary M. Comadoll to become their very own daughter.*" She belonged to them.

~ ~ ~

Like all other closed adoptions, my records were sealed at this point. I became number 143520, filed away in the impressive Confederation Building. Promises had been made to the birth mother to never reveal her identity. Promises were made to my adopted parents never to reveal their identity. Both parties truly believed that in the interest of everyone, including me, this was the "right," "honorable," and certainly the only "safe" way to handle my adoption. That was just the way things were done in the '50s.

~ ~ ~

From an objective, calculated perspective this philosophy does make sense: birth mother makes mistake, gives her baby for adoption; it all remains a secret. Her life moves on, she forgets, no one is the wiser. Adoptive parents fear the idea that at any time in the future, the past can reach into their arms and take their bundle of love from them. So, by all means, let's all get on with our lives. Seal those files, and wrap the past in a shroud of secrets. Never mind the jumble of emotions that begins a life-long process of working themselves out in the adoptive triad. Life must go on. And as players on a stage we each assume our role, enjoying (or making the best of) life.

No one reckoned with the fact that 30, 40, even 50 years later the desire to *KNOW* who we are would resurface for so many adoptees. Many of our stories are good. We aren't emotionally scarred, we count our blessings, and we have nothing to be ashamed of or to hide. But we do have a compelling desire to know *WHO* we are. Who shares the same genetic palette? People who have always had this information, or can get it with just a casual question, have no idea how much tiny scraps of information can mean to an adoptee. In the meantime, locked in cellars, musty offices and mildewed cardboard boxes lay precious secrets for which thousands of adoptees would pay nearly any price. We are driven by the simple question, WHO am I?

Official United States visa picture

One month later on June 7, 1952, the little Newfie came to America. When the family crossed the border, I had a Canadian passport. For his final tour of duty, Daddy was granted his request to be stationed at the Greater Pittsburgh military base. For me, it was a new family, a new town, a new community, and a new home at Haribson's Trailer Court in Oakdale, Pennsylvania, for the next five years.

One of my favorite childhood pastimes was to listen to stories my mother would tell me about the places where she and Daddy had lived in the military. Homesickness was not an ever-present, ongoing problem for her, but she had her share. Being stationed at Pittsburgh meant that for the first time she was close to her family, only forty-five miles away from Brownsville, Pennsylvania. Most weekends were spent at Grandma and Grandpa's house. We would leave on Friday when Daddy got off work and return Sunday afternoon. Following Daddy's retirement, the Comadoll family moved permanently to Brownsville.

Aunts, uncles, cousins and, of course, Grandma and Grandpa were always around making up the family hub. Without any hesitation, the entire family accepted the new baby into their family circle.

November 15, 1955, was one of the most important days of my early life. I became a naturalized citizen of the United States under petition number 158443. The Soldiers and Sailors Hall looms in my mind as being a big room with a huge table and bright lights. With approximately 300 other immigrants, Joylene Irene Comadoll declared her allegiance to the United States of America.

Then and now, I am happy to be an American. No one could be more patriotic nor respond on a

Treasured newspaper clipping

more deeply emotional level to the American flag than I. After all, my adopted daddy spent nearly forty years in the American military, with the U.S. Marines, the U.S. Army, and finally the U.S. Air Force. My birth father served in the Navy. Patriotism runs strong and deep, but on the inside, I've always been keenly aware that first I am Canadian and, most specifically, a Newfie! Over forty years would pass before my feet stepped on Newfoundland soil and I went "home" to "my people."

Proud new citizen

6

A "MIXED BAG" OF CHILDHOOD MEMORIES

The lines are fallen unto me in pleasant places;
Yea, I have a goodly heritage
(Psalm 16:6).

"No, no, no!" I screeched. "I'm not going to wear those ugly, heavy, long stockings back to school this afternoon." It was almost summer and the school days seemed to be getting longer. I wanted to be free, and one small step to that freedom was to shed those hot stockings.

"Oh, yes, you are. And furthermore, don't speak to me like that, I'm your mother," Mom replied, raising her voice a bit.

"No, you're *not* my mother. I have another mother somewhere in the world, and if she were here, she wouldn't make me wear those horrible stockings! And I don't have to listen to you; you're not my real mother!"

With eyes flashing, the words came like daggers out of my mouth. I ran out the door and down the street, in a state of sheer horror at what had just happened. The words hung suspended in mid-air—I could almost see them. What had I just done? I had never said such a despicable thing in all of my life, and certainly not to someone who loved me so completely as my mother.

Obviously, I must have been very frustrated that day. I don't remember if I finally did wear the long, hot stockings she told me to wear, or if I truly did go barelegged back to school. But I do remember that it was only a matter of hours until my smitten conscience urged me to make amends. I humbly returned to ask forgiveness for such an unkind outburst. That was the first and only time that the adoption issue ever entered a negative discussion.

Adoption was always a positive in our home. My parents must have said all the right things, and I must have heard all the right things. Yes, I was special. Yes, I had been chosen. God had a special plan for me. I was unique; I was different. In our home, the adoption issue wasn't something talked about all of the time; it was like a beautiful heirloom that sits on the mantelpiece. We knew it was there, but it didn't need tended to every day. My mother probably smiled every time she heard her little girl among the neighborhood kids. "I'm special," I would proudly proclaim. "My dad and mom wanted me. You don't know if your mom and dad wanted you or not." How insensitive could I get! But, honestly, that was how I've always accepted my adoption.

Birthdays were the one exception. My seventh birthday was the day when I finally comprehended what adoption was all about. It wasn't a negative understanding, but for many years to come my birthday would be a traumatic day. After opening my presents early in the day, I would wander away in the afternoon to ponder in solitude. *Somewhere out there in the world there's a woman who gave birth to me. Does she remember this day, December 30, as the day? Does she care? Does she ever think about me? What's her life like? What would my life be if she hadn't given me away?* This mood would last several hours, then I would return to the routine of my life, until my next birthday appeared on the calendar.

To my knowledge, my parents never read the first word about how to handle an adopted child. They just lived and loved. In retrospect, I believe one of the most important things they did was to allow me unhindered access to my past. The legal documents were filed where I could look at them any time I chose. The 8mm films taken when we were in Newfoundland entertained me many afternoons. The flag which I received on the day of my naturalization was tattered and torn, with its base and stem missing, but its message was loud and clear—I was an American! I freely touched, experienced, talked and thought about my past anytime I wanted, without ever fearing rejection from my parents or myself feeling that I had caused them pain or awkwardness. All these tangible reminders heightened my sense of security. I was me. I was special. Look, here's proof! Unanswered questions were no big deal because I had an identity, which I could enjoy anytime I chose. No small gift.

Just recently I have become aware of the incredible "match" job that God did with my personality. Being of Irish descent, with plenty of spunk, God gave me an adopted mother with a very laid-back personality. I shudder to think what life would have been like if we both had had strong per-

Bright-eyed, spunky child

sonalities. She allowed me the freedom to roam the hills and the creeks and to explore nature with a minimum of hassle. My "Newfieness" was never squelched, although I'm sure she wondered at times what made me tick. It wasn't until many years later that I discovered I'm simply an uprooted Newfoundlander. We think differently. Our brains process information in our own unique way. Newfoundlanders are not particularly interested in conforming to the "boxes" dictated by society. They have their own lives, their own sense of right and wrong. An unspoken understanding is, "you live your life, I'll live mine." Mutual respect, privacy and independence are simply lived outside the "box." They wouldn't have it any other way. These characteristics remained pretty much intact for me, thanks to the design of my loving heavenly Father.

~ ~ ~

Anthropologists tell us there is a strange and unique similarity between Newfoundland and southwestern Pennsylvania. Perhaps it is the heavy Irish migration which settled in both areas. Maybe it is the ruggedness of the people from both locations who are only a few generations away from the "old country." Without a doubt, both have some of the hardest-working, family-oriented, enduring people you will ever find. Interestingly, these two worlds even look and feel alike!

St. John's, Newfoundland, boasts having the first street in North America. John Cabot brought the European civilization to Newfoundland just a few years before Columbus discovered America. A deep sense of history is associated with this town. The same is true for Brownsville, Pennsylvania. It isn't difficult to find old Indian relics scattered along the banks of the Monongahela River. Then came the early days of America, with George

Washington traveling Route 1 and crossing the first iron-cast bridge built in America, located right on Main Street in Brownsville. Every day on my way to junior high school, I would pass Nemicoln Castle, built during the late 1700s. Brownsville was reportedly one of the main arteries of the south-going-north slave routes of the Civil War. Brownsville's bicentennial in 1965 carried with it a sense of mysterious history. The coke ovens, company houses, coal tipples, barges and railroad roundhouses all lent their own special spice to life. I love the historical and cultural diversity of Brownsville. It is more than just a "place," it has "presence."

The fact that my parents were older when they adopted me had both its positives and negatives. In some ways, it was more like being raised by grandparents than parents. They always had time for me. My wish was their command. I could always count on winning when Daddy played games with me. My mud pies were the best in town, the pencil scribble the best ever done. And I was the most outstanding bike rider in town—so said my daddy. It really didn't matter what the occasion, Daddy was my ever-present cheerleader through life. Together, this all did wonders for self-esteem!

But life wasn't all fairy tales with no pain. One could not understand the full and true picture of my life if it was not known that, in today's terms, our home would be called "dysfunctional." Both my parents treated me with incredible love, yet they forgot to love each other. Perhaps it was because, for the first time, my mother lived near her family, and my father could not handle such close contact. Maybe it was because Daddy seemed able to love only one person at a time, and his love was transferred from my mom to me. Several years after his death, I was stunned to read that while he had been in the military, he had been diagnosed as schizophrenic. Certainly that information gave insight to the bizarre actions that he sometimes exhibited. I was the "shuttle" between two very unhappy people whose lives wrapped me in a cocoon of love, yet whose own lives were emotionally starved. Many, many nights I cried myself to sleep in sheer frustration.

Once, their fighting became so intense that I packed my little bundle of things, fully intending to live the rest of my life at my friend's house. She listened to me, wiped my tears, and convinced me that I should go back home. I would only bring more pain to both parents if I wasn't there.

Because of my parents' fractured relationship, I was the sun, moon and stars to each of them. Their entire world revolved around me. That's fine, to a point, but ultimately it's a heavy burden for a child to bear. The success of holidays, especially Christmas, rested on my small shoulders. I tried so desperately to "buy" them happiness. Yet to this day, I'm confident they never meant it to be that way. They were beautiful, big-hearted people who gave me so much more than my share. I loved them so much and would have done anything to wipe away the pain in their eyes, yet I never could. There are scars, wounds, and memories I will forever carry with me, but even through it all, I never resented the fact that adoption had "put" me in those circumstances.

Given the unhappy emotional chemistry of my home, I was always rather glad to have my own set of genes. Strange as it may sound, because I didn't know that cancer might run in my family, or that family members died early from heart disease, or

Grandma and Grandpa Taylor along with me and one of my favorite bunny rabbits

that any one of a hundred other physical ailments were part of my family tree, somehow I developed the idea that I was immortal. Other people had bad diseases to worry about, but because I didn't know of any, I thought I was disease free. A rather "freeing," but unrealistic way to look at life.

Despite the emotional turmoil that swirled around my life, nearly all my childhood memories are neat. My list of pets would rival the list of a zoo. Many years later I would learn that many adoptees relate closely with animals. No one worried much about bedtimes or mealtimes at our house—we just kinda went with the flow. A big bowl of strawberry shortcake, Spanish rice, or a good mess of corn and beans made for a wonderfully delicious meal, anytime we wanted it. Report cards were a mixed bag—the grades weren't too bad, but the "talks-too-much" got me in big-time trouble!

"Joylene, have your practiced your piano lesson today? "

"Yes, Mom."

"How long?"

Dropping my mouth into my elbow, hoping she couldn't understand my muffled answer, I would reply, "About five minutes."

My favorite way to practice the piano

"Five minutes! You know your teacher said you needed to practice at least half an hour a day, and I think it should be more like an hour!"

"I know, I know." And I did know, but I didn't *care*. I would purposely put the clock in another room, then when the time needed to be checked, I would have a wonderful excuse to trot around the house and get off that dreadful bench.

From the first day my mom held me and saw my long slender fingers, she dreamed of my music accomplishments—a dream I never shared! Oh, I loved music, but I wanted to do it my *own* way.

"Now, Joylene," my teachers would admonish, "you put in extra notes. What you just played isn't written there."

"I know, but doesn't it sound pretty? Why can't I do it like I want to? I think the way I play is just as pretty as the way they wrote it." And around and around we would go.

"Sure, go ahead, write down the assignment in my assignment book, but if you think I'm going to practice this boring song, think again. I don't like it; I won't practice it; it's too boring!" That's some of the dialogue my poor teachers and mother struggled with through years of piano, organ and accordion lessons.

Perhaps I did have some musical talent, but all those *assigned* hours of practice (which never materialized!) didn't match my free-spirited outlook on life. And besides, when spring has just sprung, who in her right mind wanted to be cooped up inside! The world was waiting to be explored! On rainy days, Nancy Drew books were waiting to be read; Barbie dolls wanted to be played with; or my play "office" needed to be organized. I loved to collect John F. Kennedy cards, and that took a fair share of time also.

The neighborhood kids and I enjoyed the seasons—each of them! During the winter, we went sledding and ice skating and built snowmen. The first hint of spring found me wandering in the woods, looking for the first signs of my beloved green world. Pansy planting was a ritual. In the days before animal rights, our local dime store sold live bunnies, peeps and ducks for Easter. Deciding which animal would be my Easter pet and actually choosing and taking one home was so much fun. When summer came, the long, hot, beautiful days ended in hide-and-seek or firefly catching. Fall came and it was back to the classroom. My life moved in a beautiful rhythm, and I enjoyed it to

Our family at one of Daddy's re-enlistment ceremonies

the fullest. Someone has said, "Make memories—they will be your roses in old age." I already
have a beautiful bouquet!

7

A RICH HERITAGE

He that dwelleth in the secret place of the most high
shall abide under the shadow of the Almighty (Psalm 91:1).
Under whose wings thou art come to trust (Ruth 2:12).

Check(✔), check(✔), check(✔). Three more classes finished and checked off. The date could have read any number of days on the calendar—it really didn't matter. Through most of my junior and senior high school years, I enjoyed this checking-off ritual in anticipation of attending my beloved camp meeting.

Camp meeting—maybe that's why I always looked forward so much to summer. Summertime to me meant we packed and traveled 120 miles north to a little grove of trees overlooking Sandy Lake, located in a little town called Stoneboro, Pennsylvania.

Just the words "camp meeting" evoke an image of bygone days. Camp meetings, for many, are a relic of religious gatherings left over from the early twentieth century. But for me, our camp meeting was alive and well and definitely the high-light of my year. Modern-day health and safety people would have been absolutely horrified to walk through some of those dorms. And it didn't help much to hear the adults talk about how fast a fire could sweep through those buildings. With the old wooden structures about a hundred years old, we would have been trapped with not a ghost of a chance of escaping should a fire ever happen. But that was the only anxious thought. The musty smell of buildings which had been closed up all winter, drawing water at the well, washing in buckets, sleeping on lumpy mattresses, living by a rigid schedule, and sitting on hard benches for endless hours didn't seem a hardship at all. These were my people, and, best of all, the presence of God was there.

My impressionable years of childhood were filled with Bible and character stories in the "Children's Tabernacle." Fundamental Christian doctrines such as sin and its consequences were firmly, yet lovingly, taught. Early understanding of God the Creator, Jesus the Good Shepherd, and God my best Friend were shaped at these gatherings. Evening services were a bit more dramatic when older, white-haired ministers thundered forth the truth of God. Above everything else, they challenged us to a deeper walk with God. To know God was the highest pursuit and privilege of mankind. There was something clear, pure and refreshing about not only their words, but also their lives. During my teen years, we heard much about the coming "rapture" of Christ for His Church. Oh, how I wanted to be ready!

The world at large of the late '50s and early '60s was interesting. Those were the days of the Cold War. Khrushchev thundered and bragged about the Russians burying us alive. This was not exactly a comforting thought! I well remember one night going to my neighbor's home to find her engrossed in listening to the radio. Since my parents never kept current in world events, I had no clue to what was so important. I asked her what was happening and was quickly told that right then, even as we sat safely tucked away in our secure Pennsylvania world, the world was 'fixin' to blow up any minute!" Ships were loaded with missiles enroute from Russia to Cuba, and President Kennedy had issued the ultimatum that those ships must turn around. Hour after hour they steamed closer and closer to Cuba. I was terrified! I ran home to tell my parents of the impending doom and begged them to reconcile their differences so we all could depart in peace. What relief to learn that Khrushchev changed his mind and the ships had turned around! But to say that the Cold War made an interesting backdrop to living is to put it very mildly.

Many trips were made to the altar to make sure my relationship with God was right. Obviously, neither the Rapture nor a Communist takeover has yet happened, but the impact of this style of preaching and the realities of my childhood have shaped my life, giving me a healthy respect for an up-to-date relationship with God.

As important as the services were, the social connections made at camp meeting were also significant. Like no other place on earth, this small, conservative group of holiness people could feel connected. Our traditions were understood, appreciated, and passed down to the next generation, under the watchful eyes of our elders. Stoneboro Camp Meeting was a haven for our little band of people! We were there only 21 days out of the year, however. The rest of the year was lived as "pilgrims and strangers in this world."

Our Wesleyan Methodist roots extend back to John Wesley and the Methodist church. Over the years when issues arose, they usually played themselves out from a "liberal" or "conservative" viewpoint. Inevitably, as issues arose, our little band of pilgrims chose the more conservative route.

These issues had an interesting way of being played out in daily living. Our church leaders taught that we should be modest, and certainly, modesty for women meant dresses. First Corinthians 11:6 calls for a woman to have a covering of long hair, that is neither shorn nor shaven. Therefore, women did not cut their hair. Keeping the Sabbath Day holy means exactly that. You don't buy or sell. Sunday is a day of rest. Popular forms of entertainment were taboo: movies, gambling, rock concerts, and television.

Naturally, all this teaching and the nurturing of a close personal relationship with God translated into a very careful lifestyle. Yes, I was made fun of at times because my dresses went below the knee (even during the mini-skirt era), but that was our faith. Perhaps there was a connection between being "different" because of my adoption and being "different" for my faith. Any way you look at it, I was just plain different. But that was okay. I'm me, and my Drummer has always given me a different tune by which to march.

Some consider our standards of dress and lifestyle as "externals," but more importantly and influential has been the "internal" foundation of faith. God has always been real to me, and His presence has always been desired and never feared. He is my loving heavenly Father. Modern Christian psychology tells us that our view of God is based on our relationship and view of our earthly father. During my formative years (before I became aware of our family deficiencies), Daddy was my hero. He gave me unconditional love and steadfastly supported my smallest accomplishment. He was forgiving, kind, and keenly interested in everything of interest to me. I was always confident he wanted only the best for me, and he moved heaven and earth to make the best come true. God, my heavenly Father, is just like my daddy, only to a much greater degree.

~ ~ ~

"Suppertime. You all come and get a bite to eat," called Mom from the kitchen. No one had to be called twice; Daddy and I were always hungry. But this evening something was different. Mom had cooked the food, put it on the table and called us to eat, but she had disappeared. What was going on? I went to her room, where the door was open enough so that I could peek. Much to my dismay, not only was she skipping supper, but she was praying. I knew what the problem was!

Although I had grown up in a Christian (though dysfunctional) home, I had never truly given my heart and life to Christ. I was in the seventh grade now, with the pressures of public school beginning to confront my "differentness." It was time. Time for me to seek a personal relationship, a born-again experience, with Christ. My mother couldn't have gone about it any better way. Prayer changes things, and prayer quickly melted my stubborn, independent heart. Shortly afterward, I knelt at an altar of prayer.

Kneeling at an altar was certainly not a new experience, but this time was different. This time I wasn't praying a child's prayer of "Now I lay me down to sleep." This prayer was a prayer of repentance and commitment, an adult decision to follow Christ. The simple ABCs of the gospel became a reality to me: I *asked* Jesus to come into my life, I *believed* He would keep His promise and make me His child, and I *confessed* my sins. For the most part, my outward appearance would not change, but on the inside I was adopted into the family of God. My birth mother's simple request that I be placed in a religious, Protestant home had certainly been granted.

8

"WELL DONE, MY FAITHFUL SERVANTS"

Great is Thy Faithfulness! Great is Thy Faithfulness
Morning by morning new mercies I see.
All I have needed thy hand hath provided.
Great is Thy faithfulness, Lord, unto me!
(Chorus—Thomas O. Chisholm)

When exactly does a child become an adult? Who knows? But somewhere along the way it happened to me as it happens to everyone. If you will read books written on adoption, you will learn that simply because day follows day, month follows month, and year follows year, adoptees *do* grow up. In most of the writings, you will also find unresolved issues. Wounds and hurts, scabbed and scarred, lay in the shadows behind what appears to be normal functioning adults. Whether identified or unidentified, this reality continues to have an impact, both in subtle and not-so-subtle ways nearly every day of their lives. It doesn't matter that their lives are molded either "because of" or "in spite of," adoptees have the same opportunities as everyone else to grow and mature.

In retrospect, I believe that upon entering my adult life, I was given the best of both worlds. From my Newfie birth mother, I inherited a rich genetic heritage. My adoptive parents gave me incredible love and opportunity to be myself, and provided me with a unique, yet beautiful framework from which God could easily speak to me. This is not to say that my birth mother would have done any less or that my adoptive parents were superior (or vice versa). It simply says this was how my path twisted and turned, and I have no regrets.

The intervening years between my childhood and age forty have been an incredible journey. Graduation from high school and my first date came about the same time. John Budensiek is the most beautiful gift that God has given me. After three years of dating, we were married. Three children—Julie; John, Jr.; and Jim—completed our family. Our move to Florida meant striving for and accomplishing more goals.

My adoptive daddy passed away first, then my mom. Because my adoption took place in their middle years, the clock of life ticked faster for our time together as a family. Both died with cancer, which by its very nature meant there was time for reflection, confessions, and heart-wrenching moments. But none came forth on *any* subject. This included my adoption, a topic that still didn't surface when life itself was most solemn and reflective.

As so often happens, adversity brings out the best in people. When Daddy's health began to fail, my parents seemed to again find each other after many years of emotional upheaval. But in spite of witnessing a healing in their marriage, questions haunted me about Daddy's relationship with his God. Had he truly made his peace? Did he fully comprehend what it meant to know Christ? I had to know, so one afternoon I determined to ease my mind.

Entering the small travel trailer parked near our home, I gathered the courage to ask, "Daddy, if something should happen to you, have you made your peace with God?"

Straightening his shoulders and looking me in the eye with a puzzled expression, he replied in his gravelly voice, "If I wasn't, don't you think I'd be doing something about it?"

"Yes, of course." That was the beginning and the end of the conversation. In my mind the matter was settled.

A few days later, surrounded by his family, Jack Comadoll took his last earthly breath. I imagined God giving two trustworthy angels the special assignment to bring one of His children home.

"Gabriel, Michael, I have a special assignment for you today. There is a tired soldier down in Jupiter, Florida, who only I understand—no one else could. On your softest angel wings, go down and bring him home to Me—his mission is completed."

I don't really know, of course, if this was played out in heaven, but each of us in the room that day will testify that angels truly did come. Their presence was felt so strongly that I actually looked to the corners of the room to see if they were visible. They were not. It wasn't necessary to see them with the human eye. We all just knew.

Daddy died on a Saturday. What do you do the morning after a death in the family? We always went to church on Sundays, but that Sunday it didn't seem quite right so we stayed home. I shall never forget my husband sitting at the piano playing the tried and tested songs of our faith. One song in particular caught my ear—

"Great Is Thy Faithfulness"

Great is Thy faithfulness, O God, my Father;
There is no shadow of turning with Thee.
Thou changest not; Thy compassions, they fail not.
As Thou hast been Thou forever wilt be.

Pardon for sin and a peace that endureth,
Thy own dear presence to cheer and to guide,
Strength for today and bright hope for tomorrow
Blessings all mine, with ten thousand beside!

God inaudibly spoke to me that morning, giving spiritual insight into His great loving heart: *Joy, you have experienced My love, and you've seen Me at work. Yesterday I took special care of your daddy—the daddy that no one understood; the man who was locked in his own emotional abyss, with no one having a key. I loved him. He had a special relationship with Me, though people looking on could not see it. My love goes farther; My understanding is more inclusive than you are able to discern. I have compassion for those whom society casts off as unsociables. They, too, are created in My image. In his inner heart, your daddy loved Me and did his best to serve Me. Remember that Jack Comadoll is not the only person in your world who doesn't seem to "fit," but they all are Mine. My compassions fail not. They are new every morning, and great is My faithfulness!*

Daddy taught me a lot in my growing-up years, but perhaps the glimpse into God's unfathomable love was his final and best lesson to me.

Six years later, Mom, too, succumbed to cancer. Together, we made the trips to chemotherapy, and together we rejoiced when the side effects weren't too bad. Her one wish that she not lose her hair was granted. God is so good! Once, during a reflective moment, Mom said, "It's not the dying I'm afraid of. It's just the path between now and then."

A few months before she passed on, I felt that she, in her own words, summed up her own mission in life. She had been reading in Matthew 26 where Mary had poured her alabaster box of ointment on the head of Jesus, wanting it to be a blessing. Her comment was, "I do hope my life is a perfumed blessing to everyone I know."

Mom's life was a blessing. Her personal unfilled dreams for a child and her own tears and heartaches were taken by a God Who truly worked all things together for our good. This was the back-drop for the drama in my own life.

Life moves on. Studies on adoptions indicate that after we adoptees have had our own child-raising experiences and our nests begin to empty, our minds begin to remind us that our own clock is ticking. It was time to tackle the one huge unresolved issue in life. So, along with thousands of other adoptees, I began my search. I had no clue to the winding, twisting road of highs and lows that was about to begin, nor how long the drama would last.

9

IN THE CLOUDS FOR DAYS

I will instruct thee and teach thee in the way
Which thou shalt go;
I will guide thee with mine eye
(Psalms 32:8).

"Joy," questioned a colleague, "have you heard about the cheap airline tickets on sale right now?"

"No, what are you talking about?"

"Well, most of the big airlines are having a special where you can go round-trip anywhere in the United States for only $129. Not bad, huh?"

No, not bad at all. For someone like myself who enjoys and thrives on travel, it sounded too good to pass up. Where could we go? Ah! My husband and I had talked on and off many times about going to Newfoundland.

"When does the ticket sale end?"

"I think today." If I was going to act, it had to be fast!

Without telling another soul, I drove to the travel agency and asked for the destination that would come closest to Newfoundland. Portland,

Maine—yes, that would work. We would rent a car and go from there. "Okay, I'd like two tickets. One for Joy Budensiek, the other for John Budensiek." John, meanwhile, was innocently sitting in his accounting office, having no clue of the adventure coming his way.

With tickets in hand, off I went to find my unsuspecting husband. Fortunately, though, we had talked enough about it beforehand that he wasn't totally blown away with the idea; and, in fact, seemed rather pleased to have the vacation decision settled.

One would think that with all of my dreams and fantasies I would have had a better grip on the actual distances. I didn't. We flew to Portland, rented a car, and drove to Nova Scotia, with plans to take a plane from Nova Scotia to Newfoundland. When we arrived in the Halifax airport, ready to buy our tickets, we discovered that Newfoundland was far more than a hop, skip and jump—and the prices reflected that distance.

"Now what'll we do?" we asked each other. "We've come all this way to go to Newfoundland, but we don't have money like this! And we can't drive; it will take too many days."

I'll never forget the moment. We both felt the presence of the Lord and heard Him speak in an almost audible voice: *I don't want you to go to Newfoundland. I want you to enjoy Nova Scotia.* There was an unexplainable peace that came over both of us. We were confident that God was in control.

It was so easy to just "chill." No anxiety, but simply a rest which could have come only from God. It was so great to be in Canada, with an entire week to spend in Nova Scotia. *I may not be able to get all the way to Newfoundland on this trip, but I'm getting closer than I've ever been before,* I thought. As we met people while leisurely touring the province, I would put on a big smile and proudly say, "I'm from Newfoundland. Do you know anybody from Newfoundland?" Innocent me! Unbeknownst to me, for some Canadians, Newfoundland is considered the bottom rung of society. I did this many times, receiving a variety of responses. But, like all my fellow Newfies, I was a proud Newfie. (Newfoundlanders do consider themselves special. We would never think of being anything else, regardless of other people's perception!)

Liverpool, located on the southern side of Nova Scotia, is a beautiful resort town catering to tourists. We had never been there before—had never heard of it, but as the night shadows began to creep in, we knew it was time to be looking for a place to spend the night. A typical bed-and-breakfast sign caught our eye. How about a little cultural experience for the night?

Yes, there was a room available; and, yes, we could rent it for one night. An advantage to staying at a bed-and-breakfast is the interaction you have with the people. They are generally outgoing, sociable personalities who enjoy sharing not only their facilities, but also their lives. These people were eager to talk. As usual, Newfoundland was mentioned, and they were told how our original plans went awry.

"Newfoundland, huh?" the gentleman said, raising his eyebrows. "I'm from St. John's, Newfoundland."

"Oh, my goodness," I exclaimed. "I am too!"

"Why do you want to go there?"

"I'm adopted. I'm trying to find my roots."

"Wow! How old are you? When is your birthday?"

When I told him my age and birthday, he actually counted on his fingers and, looking at me with a smile, said, "I'm not your dad." His wife, who was intently listening to this exchange was not impressed in the least. And judging from her facial expression, I was also happy he wasn't my father!

"But I tell you what," he continued, "I'm a retired pilot, and I go back and forth between Nova Scotia and Newfoundland all the time. My brother works as a clerk of court where your records are sealed. Would you like me to help you open your records?"

Oh, God! I've never been in this town before. I don't even know these people! Is this what you had in mind? Have you directed our steps 2,000 miles from home to this man's doorstep? Wow, Lord, You are so good to me! I was overwhelmed. I was ecstatic! God was working on my behalf!

"*Can* you? Will you?"

We finished our vacation and returned to Florida. Duplicates were made of my adoption papers and sent to our friends at the bed-and-breakfast.

Correspondence began between myself and the Newfoundland social services. It wasn't long before I received a brown envelope from their office in St. John's. (Brown envelopes became a welcome trademark that I learned to appreciate early on.)

Forty years of absolute silence is a long time. Was I ready to break that silence by opening this brown envelope postmarked "St. John's, Newfoundland?" I held that letter for a long time without opening it. (Most adoptees know that indescribable feeling—lots of excitement with equal doses of fear—excitement about everything, fear about everything.) Finally, taking a very deep breath, I willed my fingers to open it. My life would never be the same.

November 1992

Dear Joy:

We have received a request for this information and we have researched your files. We are experiencing a back-log of cases, and it may be some time before we can begin a search for your mother. Here is some non-identifying information which you may find useful:

- Your mother is a native Newfoundlander.
- She was 25 years old at your birth.

- She was a clerk.
- She is average height with a medium complexion.
- She was an attractive, pleasant person.
- Her religion was the Salvation Army.
- Prior to your birth, she resided in a home for unwed mothers.
- Following your birth, she remained at the Home until you were placed with an adoptive family.
- She and her family have always been in good health.
- She is of British descent.
- Your father was tall, dark and handsome. (Just like the man of my dreams!)
- He was in the American navy.
- He had no physical or emotional problems to your mother's knowledge. (What a relief!)
- Your mother did not name your birth father and paternity was not legally established.

Sincerely yours,

I was in the clouds for days. I had one single piece of paper which gave me a clue to who I was! Those who have always known who they are and where they're from cannot begin to grasp the importance of a few scraps of "identifying information." In genealogy, it's called your "pedigree." I hate that word! (I had always associated that word with dogs and cats.) But now, for the first time, I was beginning to learn my pedigree, and it was intensely important. I truly *did* have a mother! I truly *did* have a father! They were flesh and blood, just like me! *That simple piece of paper was pure gold!*

Application was made for a search, but I was told it would take many years before my file came to the top for review. So we settled down to wait—someday, sometime, somehow. Life went on.

I could not recall ever having met a person from the Salvation Army, but now my antennae were activated; I listened to any reference made about these people. The Army made a significant contribution to my life, and I had to know more about them!

That year I was assigned cafeteria hostess at the camp meeting in Hobe Sound, Florida. My attention was particularly drawn toward a beautiful little lady who took her meals in the cafeteria. Imagine my surprise when I learned she was a major in the Salvation Army! She was a delightful person. Before long, we, like Anne of Green Gables, discovered we were "kindred spirits"! Our conversations roamed from the mountains of Central America to the cities of Europe. It seemed to me that she and her husband had been missionaries all over the world.

"By the way," I casually asked, "have you ever been to Newfoundland?"

"Have I ever been to Newfoundland! Oh, yes, honey, I spent *time* up there!" *Oh, my goodness! Here we go again, God!*

"You've gotta be kidding! Do you know anything about a home for unwed mothers there?"

"Oh, yes, the Army had a home for unwed mothers. Some of my friends used to work there." (It was maddening how nonchalant she was about such an important subject.)

"Well, I think I was born at that home. Could you . . . would you," I stammered, "be interested in helping me do some research? Do you still have friends in high places?"

"Oh, yes, I have friends."

"Oh! Would you please write up there and see if you can find out anything? I was born December 30, 1951. . . . " I told her everything I knew.

She wrote to her friends, and they replied in record time: "We have on our records that a female baby was born on December 30, 1951." That was it—period.

Now I knew exactly *where* I was born! Another piece was in place. God's clock keeps perfect time, and slowly but surely, it continued to tick.

10

THANKS, BUT NO THANKS

Though He giveth or He taketh
God His children ne'er forsaketh.
His the loving purpose solely
To preserve them pure and holy
(Caroline V. Sandell-Berg).

Ring-a-ling, ring-a-ling. In the days before caller identification, I had no clue that answering the phone would give me earth-shattering information. It just rang like it always did.

"Hi, my name is Lydia Arnold. I'm from the social services of St. John's, Newfoundland. Are you Joy Budensiek?"

"I am; I really am!" My mind raced to catch up with my voice.

"Your file has come to the top of hundreds of applicants looking for their families. The last contact we had with you was nearly five years ago."

"Yes, that's correct."

"Have events in your life changed? At that time you wanted us to conduct a search for your mother. Do you still want us to work on locating your mother? Do you want us to do a search?"

"I do! I do! I really do!" I was beside myself with excitement.

"Well, I'll call you back tomorrow and get more information from you."

"Can't I give it to you today? I probably already know the answers to everything you're going to ask me. Can't I give it to you today?" I didn't want to wait another minute!

"Well, yes, I guess we can do it now."

She went through sheets of questions. My records were being updated so when contact was made with my mother, they would have something to tell her. I was shaking when I laid down the phone. *Dear Lord, what am I doing?*

October 1998. Our lives were careening down the hectic path of living. Our three children were nearly grown and branching into lives of their own. Good, clean, fulfilling lives, both for them and us. My husband and I had careers we enjoyed. Our mortgage was nearly half paid. Yes, life was good. But not complete. Months went by without reference being made to my adoption search, but it was always and forevermore tucked away in my mind and heart. Now this phone call had come and with it an uncertain future. The secrets of a lifetime were about to be learned. How exciting! How fearful!

When I went to bed that night, I was tingling with anticipation. "I just have this gut feeling, Hon, this feeling in my bones, that my mama is not far off." My husband was with me in this all the way. Turning out the light and snuggling into the comfort of bed, I knew it wouldn't be long.

Newfoundland is an hour and a half (that's right, an hour and a half!) *ahead* of Florida. (Newfies do things differently, including the time zones!) Before Floridians are awake, Newfoundlanders have put in a half morning of work. Before I had my eyes open the next morning, the phone was ringing.

"Joy, I found your mother!" Lydia's voice shared in the excitement of the moment.

"Oh, you found her!" I squealed. "What did she say? Does she want to talk to me? Can we make connections?" I rapid-fired questions to her.

"Now just calm down," she said. "These things are very delicate, very sensitive. You must remember that most of the women who were involved in these situations are in their sixties and seventies now. Back in their day, this was such a shameful thing that no one talked about it. No one in her family may have known. These girls were told to forget and go on with their lives. You are a ghost of the past that she has probably spent a lifetime trying to forget. The poor lady's in shock."

"Yes, she probably is," I agreed, sighing. But this was a new idea to me. That my mother might not *want* to connect with me simply had not occurred to me.

"She's just overwhelmed, Joy. She doesn't know what to say. She said to call her back in a couple weeks. She will have an answer then. Give her time."

Taking a deep breath, I assured Lydia that I truly would try to understand.

"But, Lydia, wait! If you're going to be talking to her again, please tell my mama that the *only* reason I want to find her is to tell her that I love her. My intentions are good, and I don't come with any baggage. I have no resentment. And please, oh, please, if you think it's a good idea, remind her that my birthday is December 30. Maybe that will be the perfect time for something to happen."

"We don't call people around the Christmas holiday season, Joy. We've found that it's not a wise thing to do. But if I have good news, I'll call and share it with you. You have my word on it."

The wait began, again. Christmastime came. I tried not to expect anything. But on the morning of my birthday, I couldn't help myself. *Today's the day!* I thought.

For the most part, I had outgrown the "birthday blues" of my childhood. Life was so busy that to spend much time in solitude and reflection was an indulgence which hadn't happened for years. But this birthday was different—never before had I felt so close to reconnecting. I wouldn't leave the house, and I stayed close to the phone.

Nine o'clock. The phone rang, but it wasn't who I expected.

Ten o'clock. Tension was tight, especially when the phone rang.

Eleven . . . twelve . . . four.

Five o'clock. With a gut-wrenching pain deep in my stomach, I realized it wasn't going to happen today. She *knew* it was my birthday, but she chose not to call. I was devastated.

Two days passed before my curiosity got the best of me. I picked up the phone. "Lydia, have you heard from my mother?"

"Yes, Joy, we did. We heard from her only a few days after I talked to you. She sent a message several days before Christmas, but we didn't call you because of our policy to not communicate around the Christmas season." Oh, the pain I had experienced because of bureaucracy policy.

The wait was just a few seconds to hear her message, but I lived a lifetime. "Joy, your mother asked that we relate this greeting to you: 'I'm so glad to hear you are doing well—so am I. I'm very proud of you, and I'm glad you've had a good life. You would probably like to know a little medical history of your family. Our family has always been healthy, and most have lived until in their 70s. We do have cancer and heart problems in the family. But until a really bad disease comes along, we don't have many problems. I was only sixteen when I had you. (The information I had received said twenty-five!) The only person who knew of your birth was my mother, and she has since passed away. I wish the best for you. I will always carry you in my heart. God bless. Merry Christmas. Happy Birthday. Love, Mother.'"

Oh.

"Joy? Are you okay?" asked Lydia, concerned on the other end of the line.

"Yes, I'll be fine. Thanks for calling. You've been great trying to help me."

After hanging up the phone, I sat, stunned. *Dear God, now what do I do?*

My adoption had always been positive. I had heard other adoptees relate how rejected and unwhole they felt, but I simply could not share those feelings. Now in middle age, was I going to get hit full in the face with this? *How can she do this to me a second time? Maybe she had valid reasons for giving me up in the first place, but why can't she acknowledge my existence now? Why?*

When things get really tight in my life—I mean really tough—my favorite recourse is to go to the beach. I sit and talk to God. So to the beach I went that day. The usual warm, balmy breezes were not coming in across the Atlantic Ocean, and it was a little cool. Very few people were around. I was glad, for anyone watching would have wondered about me. When I talk to God, I *talk* with Him as I do with my family or friends. And since God is my best Friend, He hears it like it is.

"Lord, You know that I've never gone through the rejection, the hurt, or any other deeply felt emotions that some people who are adopted have experienced. I've always been okay with it, God.

But today, *today*! It's a pretty heavy-duty load I've just been given and I really need help right now."

I don't know how many hours I sat there talking to God, but, finally, I opened my little songbook. (Two special books in my life are my Bible and my small, pocket hymnal.) The old familiar hymns always speak to me, but a song I had never noticed before caught my attention and spoke to my heart:

"Children of the Heavenly Father"

Children of the Heavenly Father,
Safely in His bosom gather;
Nestling bird nor star in heaven
Such a refuge e'er was given.

God, His own doth tend and nourish
In His holy courts they flourish.
From all evil things He spares them;
In His mighty arms He bears them.

Neither life nor death shall ever
From the Lord, His children sever;
Unto them His grace He showeth
And their sorrows all He knoweth.

I cannot tell you all that happened to me that day. All I know is that the God of the universe surrounded me with the peace and love that only He can give. And on that little strip of sand on the beach in Hobe Sound, Florida, God picked me up in His arms and whispered to me: *Joy, my child, listen to Me. Your self-worth, your identity, your everything has never come from being your mother's child. Your importance does not depend on your last name. Who you are and how you live depends on your relationship with Me, and the hurt you've experienced today does not change anything. You are who you are because I love you.*

Oh. Of course! God had not dumped me! He had not turned His back on me. I was still safe and secure. Sometimes God gives, sometimes God takes, but He is still God. No bird, no star, *nothing* in the universe was more important to God than I was at that moment. I was not going through this alone. God had a purpose and a plan for every scene being played out on the stage of my life. Relax.

I left the beach with a deep assurance that God was truly in control. This bump in the road had nothing to do with rejection by Him. Once again, God turned my world right side up. From that time on, the searching for my roots was completely in the hands of my heavenly Father. I was His child and that was enough.

Did my curiosity die? No. I'm still a Newfie—and we still try to figure out what is going on! Though my heart and emotions were at rest, I still had to figure out what to do next, if anything.

Lydia had said she would call me only one more time before my records were forever, *forever* sealed. By law, I knew she could not do much more, but I wanted to get as much information from her as possible. So when her call came, I was prepared. I asked every single question that came to my mind. She was kind but efficient, and I could tell some answers were evasive.

"Tell me, Lydia, do you think there's any hope of reunion?" The conversation was coming to an end.

"No, Joy, I don't. The best you can hope for is that *IF* you have a sibling, he or she may someday contact you. You know this same adoption process happened to many children. Now, I'm not saying that you have a sibling, Joy, but in case you do, someday you may be contacted. Good-bye and God bless."

"Thank you very much, Lydia. Thank you very much indeed!"

Siblings? Sibling means brother or sister, doesn't it? Siblings! I had never thought of such a possibility! *Dear God, does this mean there might be more than one of us? If that's true, I can't just drop this. Is there someone else who needs me to bring this all together?* Well, now, what a thought!

Mama, I thought, *you don't want to talk to me, but I want to talk to you! Now just what are we going to do about this? We've got family waiting to be found and reunited. It might be over in your books, Mama, but it **isn't** in mine.*

11

OPENING DOORS

Be still and know that I am God
(Psalm 46:10).

An afternoon without a pressing schedule—how neat. Those are such a rarity that I wanted to spend it doing something out of the ordinary. How about a trip to our college library? I love books, magazines, and that new system called the "Internet," which had just been installed. Now you must understand that, ordinarily, machines and computers are not my thing. They are strictly for getting the job done. People are so much more fun. They talk, they laugh, they interact. But that January day I had some time, so I decided to try this "surfing" thing people were talking about.

I was aimlessly surfing when I came across a website called "Classifieds." I have no clue how I got there, but "Classified Travel" came on the screen. I read, "Anywhere in the United States or Canada, four hundred dollars."

Four hundred dollars! It costs seven or eight hundred dollars to go to Newfoundland! Interesting.

If I could get to Newfoundland for four hundred dollars, I would go for it! Digging a piece of scrap paper from my pocket, I scribbled down the number. I wouldn't tell anyone—this was my secret, my dream.

Later that evening, I called the number. A guy in Texas answered. I guessed he was trying to sell frequent flyer miles.

"I need a ticket from West Palm Beach, Florida, to St John's, Newfoundland."

"Newfoundland! I don't believe my ticket will go to St. Johns, Newfoundland. Nobody in the States goes to Newfoundland!"

"I'm very well aware of that. But that's where I want to go. And let me tell you why I want to go there. I have a birth mother up there somewhere, and I want to find her. I thought maybe this ticket could help me."

"No, ma'am, I'm sorry. This ticket won't go that far."

"Okay, that's fine. No problem." The door I thought was opening had closed.

The next afternoon the phone rang.

"Hi! I'm Dave. From Texas. The ticket! Remember?"

"Oh, yes, I remember."

"You know, your story really intrigued me. I called the airline, and they said they can connect with Canadian Air. You can go all the way through to Newfoundland for four hundred dollars."

Well, now, the door just opened. *Lord, could you honestly be asking me to go to Newfoundland?*

And if so, when? In the dead of winter? Whoa! This is getting scary!

Up to this point, I hadn't told anybody. You just don't go flying to Newfoundland any old time the mood strikes. It's not a cool thing to do. My husband is a kind, wonderful, orderly person of German descent who likes to do things decently and in order. Even though I do not believe in reincarnation, if there were such a thing~~if there is anyone who deserves to be reincarnated, it is he. And the next time he deserves to have a quiet, peaceable, structured life, after the ride he has had this time around! It would be no small thing for me to ask him if I could go alone to another country in the dead of winter to look for someone whose name I didn't even know.

I've had lots of ideas in my life—some really good and some I'd rather not discuss. And, yes, sometimes I share my ideas, and other times they just "wear off." But I try not to disturb my husband's peace with my every fleeting thought. Having me for a wife, however, has given him more than his share of challenges.

I had already asked God when He wanted me to go, and I felt impressed to go during our winter church conference. Most of the time, I teach school, but during conference our schedule is lighter. There wouldn't be another opportunity until summer.

Gathering all the "stupid courage" I could muster, I ventured where angels fear to tread.

"Hon . . . I have an idea."

"Hmm, so what's new?"

"I've found the greatest deal on a ticket to Newfoundland. I'd like to go."

Raising his eyebrows, John looked at me, obviously not believing what I'd just said. "You'd like to do *what*?"

"I want to go to St. John's to find my mom!"

"Now, Hon, I can't let you go trotting up there by yourself. What are you going to do, wander along the streets with your little tin cup? I can just see you walking the streets, looking into faces for a resemblance. No, I can't let you do that! And besides, it's conference time, and you know how stressful that is for me." As the organist of Hobe Sound Bible Church, he has a heavy schedule of playing the organ for our special seminars and services.

That did it. When John said it would be too stressful for him, I backed off. "Okay, if God doesn't want it to happen, no big deal. If He wants it to happen, then we'll listen to Him. Otherwise, it's in His hands!"

A day later the telephone rang. It was for my husband.

"John, this is Ann (the conference music coordinator). I really feel badly about this and hate to tell you, but we're doing something different this year. The conference speakers want to provide their own music, so we won't need you to play the organ. I hope this doesn't mess up anything for you." When John gave me Ann's message, we both looked at each other in disbelief. Under any other circumstance we wouldn't have thought much about that bit of news, but this was no ordinary time. This had *never* happened before. Was God speaking through circumstances? "You know what?" John said. "Maybe you better think about going." Door One was open.

"It doesn't look like I have much choice, do I?" I replied.

Then I silently prayed, *Lord, if You really want me to do this, do You think You could give me some money? I don't care where it comes from. I just need a little bit of money. I'll walk through the doors if You open them, but I have to know that YOU are opening these doors. If You don't, believe me, it won't be a problem to drop it. Amen.*

Interestingly, that morning, my daily calendar read, "Be still and know that I am God." *Okay, God, I will gladly be still. You and I have this little secret; I'll call it Door Two.*

All day, I was thinking, money, money, money. I went to my mailbox. No money. Evidently, I must not have looked poor enough because nobody pressed any "green stuff" into my hand that day. Before going home I went to my college mailbox, picked up an envelope containing make-up fees for some late tests that had been given weeks before. I stuck the envelope in my bag and went home. *No money today,* I thought.

Sometime that night in my subconscious sleep, God nudged my weary brain. *You prayed for money yesterday and got it in the form of those late fees. Wake up, child, and smell the roses. I am working!* Door Two was open.

Lord, I've got a cheap ticket on reserve, permission from my husband, and confirmation through money that this is Your will. But there is another loose end to tie. I need to clear this with my employer.

"Mr. Stetler, do you have any problem with me taking off during our conference? I would like to go to Newfoundland to see if I can find my birth mother."

"Go ahead, Joy. Go ahead." Door Three was open.

"Really now, Hon, what will you do when you get there?" asked my practical husband. "You don't know a living soul up there. Are you going to stand on the street corner and hitch a ride into town? How on earth will you know where to stay? What's the crime rate like?" Valid questions, certainly.

Dear God, if you want this to continue to happen, You'll have to provide some details on the other end. I really can't wander around up there without the basic needs of life covered. If You'll supply these needs, I'll consider it Door Four.

I placed a call to Tampa to talk with my Salvation Army friend whom I had met several years earlier in our campus cafeteria. Mrs. Smith assured me that she knew people who would help me. She would immediately place a call to St. John's.

It wasn't long before the phone rang. "Hello, Joy? This is Mrs. Cummings from St. John's. Our mutual friend in Tampa tells me you want to come to St. John's. We will pick you up at the airport—it's only five miles from our home. Please tell your husband not to worry one bit about you. We will be delighted to have you stay with us the entire time you're here." Door Four was open.

Once again, I witnessed God opening and closing doors, and John and I did not doubt His will. However, I continued my conversations with God. *God, You've now opened four doors. But if at any time You don't want this to happen, then I don't want it to happen.*

The last and final door was Door Five in which the plane ticket had to still be available. My contact in Texas assured me that despite several others wanting to buy the ticket, he had held it for me. I will never forget the day I went to the bank and asked for a cashier's check to be made payable to someone I knew nothing about and had no clue of his integrity. The bank teller probably thought I had taken leave of my senses. Maybe I had, but sometimes you just have to trust God. If God had brought about things this far, He was perfectly able to keep my check safe, even if the recipient turned out to be one of the worst criminals in Texas (which he wasn't!). Door Five was open.

The emotional roller-coaster was incredible. One moment I was eager: *Yes! I'm ready. Let's go for it!* Then the next moment, I thought I was crazy: *You've got to be nuts! This lady doesn't want to see you, even if you can find her. And remember, you have no clue how to do that.*

Faith and fear wrestled together. Faith won, but only because God was so close. My daily calendar gave fresh strength every day, with its ideas, thoughts and verses. The thought for January 23, 1998, read:

> Lord, still the clamor of our days,
> And calm our rushing, anxious ways;
> In silence teach us how to praise;
> Give us peace within your love.

The next day read: "See how great a love the Father has bestowed upon us, that we should be called children of God; and such we are" (I John 3:1).

January 25 was from Isaiah 42:5,6: "Who created the heavens and stretched them out, Who spread out the earth and its offspring; Who gives breath to the people on it? I am the Lord . . . I will hold you by the hand and watch over you."

The ups and downs of my roller-coaster ride were intensifying, but again the Thought for the Day spoke to my heart:

"O Love that will not let me go,
I rest my weary soul in Thee;
I give Thee back the life I owe,
That in Thine ocean depths its flow
May richer, fuller be" (George Matheson).

Sweet, peaceful rest. One is never called upon to meet alone the challenges which God gives along the journey of life. For the Christian, there is direction and purpose. "The steps of a good man (woman) are ordered by the Lord" (Psalm 37:23). Life isn't happenstance. God not only has order and design in His universe, but also in any life yielded to Him. That is not to say there are times when His children aren't overwhelmed, but in our innermost being, rest is given to those who walk in obedience to God.

Then, of all things, panic set in. Perhaps someone *should* go with me. After all, *if* I did find my mother and if she truly did refuse to see me, the emotional fallout could be bad. After talking with several family members and friends, no one was free to go. Another talk with my Commander-in-Chief gave me this assurance, "For your Father knows what things you have need of, before you ask Him" (Matthew 6:8). *Okay, Lord, if You see I need someone, You will provide.* He was monitoring the situation and could move heaven and earth to send someone to go with me—otherwise, I would be just fine within His arms of love.

12

BOTTLE IN THE SAND

And I will give thee the treasures of darkness,
And hidden riches of secret places,
That thou mayest know that I, the Lord,
Which call thee by thy name,
Am the God of Israel
(Isaiah 45:3).

How do you explain the hand of God? How do you put together circumstances that boggle the mind unless you factor in the reality of God and His care of His children? Things happen, strange things happen with no explanation other than this: God, our heavenly Shepherd, is in heaven watching out for His little ones, and in the fullness of time, His mighty arm is extended to nudge circumstances into perfect place.

What do Newfoundlanders do in the wintertime? Go to Florida, of course. Well, not everyone, but there are many who trade a couple weeks of Newfoundland's unpredictable weather for some "fun in the sun." A cruise is a popular vacation plan. Newfoundland tourists will fly to a Florida point-of-departure and join several hundred others on an ocean liner to explore the Caribbean.

One balmy, fall day the Carnival Cruise ship steamed across the crystal waters of the Atlantic Ocean, just a few miles offshore from the Port of Fort Lauderdale. On deck, Ed and Lorrie McClain were winding down their cruise to the Bahamas. Their vacation had been terrific, and they had many experiences to share with family and friends when they arrived home. There, in front of them, stood three champagne bottles, lined up in a row as though they were soldiers standing at attention, a silent testimony to the great time they had shared. Most everyone, at one time or another, has heard of notes being placed in bottles, then tossed over the sides of ships to wash ashore and be discovered years later by someone walking along the beach. Hey, why not try their hand at that?

Three champagne bottles were tossed into the Atlantic to be swept away to who dreamed where? Maybe one was caught by the Gulf Stream and churned off toward the north, eventually to wash ashore in England—who knows? Maybe one was caught in the undertow and headed south to some exotic country in South America. We do know where one went. It rode the current northwest, mostly west and toward shore, eventually landing on a pristine beach in Hobe Sound. The hand of God gently placed the bottle. His stage was in place, and it was about time for the curtain to go up.

Two of my friends, Jose and Larry, were going about their job of lawn maintenance at a private beach home in Hobe Sound. Larry, with an ever-present eagle eye for adventure, spotted a half-buried bottle in the sand. Coming to a sudden stop, Jose jumped out and grabbed the dirty, sandy bottle. Yes, there was a paper inside! Uncorking the beautifully shaped bottle, they found the note had survived the many ocean waves. Not a hint of moisture was inside. The name and address were clearly visible on the piece of paper: Ed McClain, 47 Signal Hill Road, St. John's, Newfoundland, Canada. Interesting. Nothing more, nothing less. Larry took the bottle and the note home.

"Welcome back, Larry!" Entering the sanctuary on the Sunday prior to my planned trip to St. John's on Tuesday, I spotted my friend, Larry, sitting in a pew. We chatted about his recent trip to Vietnam.

"I'll be glad to show you my pictures," he offered.

"Not this week," I replied. "I'm taking my own trip. I'm going to St. John's, Newfoundland, to look for my birth mother."

"Really? Now isn't that interesting. Joy, this is *really* strange. Jose and I were on the far end of Jupiter Island doing landscaping at a private home when I noticed a bottle sticking up out of the sand.

Jose jumped out of the truck and picked it up. You won't believe this. The note in that bottle had the address of people from St. John's, Newfoundland on it!"

"Oh, my goodness, Larry. That can't be coincidence! So many things have fallen into place about this trip. So many, in fact, it's been a little scary!"

"Do you want the note?"

"Oh my, yes! I don't know if I'll use it or not, but I think something must be happening here!" I mean, really, when you stop to think about it, what *are* the chances?

A champagne bottle . . .
From who knows where . . .
Washing ashore onto our local beach . . .
Discovered by a good friend . . .
To whom I talked mere hours before
     leaving for St. John's . . .
Containing a name and address . . .
From the very place to where I was going . . .
Two days before I was to leave!

Dear Lord, you are incredible! The *New American Webster Handy College Dictionary* defines M-I-R-A-C-L-E as either "a wonderful thing" or "an act or happening attributed to supernatural power." I tucked away the name and address.

Still, even with such obvious signs from God, I got scared. For reasons I couldn't understand, being the adventuresome person that I am, I could not shake my fear of all the unknowns I was about to face. *Oh, God,* I prayed, *I just can't help how I'm feeling. My stomach is revolting at the very sight of food and You know this just isn't like me! If this isn't Your will,* please *close the doors. I know You've opened every single one so far, but forgive my fretting.*

The day before I left, my little calendar was prophetic in its Thought for the Day. "The Lord is good" found in Psalm 100:5 was followed by, "God's love makes a difference, a shining difference in the commonplace things of life. Today, I sat between my mother and my daughter, an extraordinary place of love . . . within His love."

I'll probably never know what circumstances prompted the author to pen those words but to me, they carried a special meaning. Talk about security! This has to be the ultimate! The very God of the universe telling me just hours before looking for my mother that one day I would have the privilege of bringing together the two generations closest to me. *Wow! I worship you, Lord.*

13

READY OR NOT, HERE I COME

The Lord is my Shepherd,
I shall not want
(Psalm 23:1).

Bags were packed, including pictures. Documents that could provide proof were tucked away, just in case. God bless my husband! Kissing me the night before departure, he assured me that truly this was the hand of God; and, yes, I had better go.

Daybreak came and with it my daughter, Julie. As we traveled south to Palm Beach International Airport, I recall two conversations going on simultaneously. One, the obvious chitchat between a mother and her daughter—the other, a dialogue between my heavenly Father and His scared child. *God, this is Your last chance,* I warned Him. *If You really do not want this to happen, if I'm going on a wild-goose chase, will You* please *do something to make this car stop? You have the power to keep us from getting to the airport.* Audibly, I allowed the two conversations to intersect.

"Jewels, if this is not supposed to happen, I hope something happens to keep us from getting to the airport."

"Mom! You know, I would like my car to stay intact!"

"Yes," I rather absent-mindedly muttered. "Yes, I would too."

The car didn't break down; we didn't have a flat tire. The traffic wasn't halted with an accident. Nothing out of the ordinary happened. I boarded.

Seated on the plane, I felt as if I had crossed an invisible line. *God, You've had every chance to stop this trip and You haven't. Whatever happens now is* Your *responsibility. I will not allow any delays to annoy me. I will accept everything that happens to be according to Your timetable.* From now on, there would be no such thing as frustrations.

A deep sense of walking with God came into my spirit. This was going to be some adventure! Every earthly tie was gone. I had no one to ask for advice, only my loving heavenly Father Who does all things well. I was happy to skip along as a child who has no worries or responsibilities, because my hand was held ever so tightly in the grasp of my heavenly Father.

The flight was incredible. God put the most awesome people in the seats next to me. Someone penned the words "friends along the way," and my flight was especially blessed with them. Debra, from Ontario, ate dinner with me in Chicago. She was a new Christian and was such an encouragement. She became so excited about my unfolding drama that she wrote me a letter and enclosed all the money she had with it, handing the envelope to me when we parted.

A Norwegian gentleman sat nearby reading his *Promise Keepers' Bible*. To me, he appeared to be a big, blond-haired angel standing guard over me. Talk about angels! I had angels the entire trip!

On the flight from Montreal to Halifax, a handsome, distinguished-looking gentleman sat across the isle from me.

"Where are you going?" he inquired.

"I'm going to St. John's, Newfoundland."

"Oh? What are you going there for?"

"To find my mother."

"To *what*?"

"To find my mother."

"You don't *know* who your mother is?"

"No," I replied.

"Well, what's her name?"

"I don't know."

"You're telling me you're going to Newfoundland to find a woman whose name you don't even know?" He was aghast.

"Yep."

"Sir, I serve a God Who has already done so many miracles just to get me here."

"Well, I'm not a believer," he said.

"I am, and it's getting exciting."

"Well, if you find her, it will be nothing short of a miracle," he conceded.

I promised to share the success of my story with him someday, just to show him that my God does work miracles.

The last flight from Halifax to St. John's was on a propjet, a smaller plane whose wings are higher than the passengers' seats. Of course, God placed me right under one of those wings to assure me that I was tucked ever so tightly under His wing, safe and totally secure.

The night shadows had fallen by the time we winged our way over Newfoundland, but no country ever looked better. So many thoughts tumbled through my head, and so many emotions enveloped my heart as I looked out over the land of my birth.

From little remote settlements, lights twinkled into the night air. I imagined the stories of love and hate, courage and trauma represented by those twinkling lights. Newfoundlanders are hardy souls, made tough from a long history of disappointments, toil and heartache, as her people have worked to wrestle a living from the unforgiving North Atlantic Ocean. Descendants primarily of England and Ireland, their background is as varied as paisley print, yet nearly every family found their way to this "new found land" because of poverty, injustice, or religious discrimination in the Old Country.

That I was still thousands of feet in the air didn't matter. I connected with these people, and after more than forty years, I was coming *home*! Somewhere below were people with my name and whose gene pool I shared. Someone laughed like me and thought like me. My flesh came from her flesh, and with God's help, I would find her.

True to her word, Mrs. Cummings met me at the airport, and after skillfully leading me through the challenge of baggage claims, I found myself outside in the Newfoundland snow! A few short hours ago, I had left seventy-degree temperatures, but now my heart was too warm to notice the drop to thirty degrees. *Thank You, God, for this beautiful newly fallen snow, just in time to welcome me. You always come through on the little things that matter to me!*

14

RECONNECTING NEWFIE

Although you roam the world around,
There's no place as special
As my hometown.

Mrs. Cummings, who had kindly invited me to stay in their guestroom for the week, had called while I was still in Florida to tell me she had forgotten their guest room was booked after the first night.

After a comfortable night's sleep, the first thing on my agenda for the day would be to find a place to stay for the rest of the week. Because my budget was somewhat limited, Mrs. Cummings thought a bed and breakfast on St. John's east side would be the most practical and least expensive place to stay. There, I was given a small second-floor room, overlooking the lights of St. John's, with every convenience I could wish. I loved my little room. It provided me the privacy and freedom to come and go as I pleased. "Consider the ravens; they do not sow or reap, they have no storeroom or barn; yet God feeds them. And how much more valuable you are than birds!" (Matthew 6:26) I didn't know it then but God had placed me within four or five blocks of my mother's home!

Mrs. Cummings, bless her heart, wasn't exactly sure what to do with me next. In all probability she, like myself, had never been involved in a "woman search" before! "What would you like to do next? The mall is outside of town," she said.

"Oh, I don't want to go to the mall—we have those in Florida. The first place I'd like to go is the funeral home."

I was here on a mission. It seemed to me that the first place to begin should be the local funeral homes. Like our own communities, people of different ethnic and religious backgrounds tend to use the services of the local funeral home which most reflects themselves. And as in Ireland, the "great divide" for Newfoundlanders is religion—Protestant or Catholic. Judging by the desire of my mother that I should be placed in a Protestant home, I assumed her to be Protestant.

"Oh . . . okay." Mrs. Cummings most definitely didn't understand this request, but off we went to Duker's Funeral Home, a Protestant establishment. Pulling up out front and stepping into the snow, I waved my friend on her way, assuring her I would be fine. She should not worry; God would take care of me.

I found the funeral home tastefully decorated. The parlor had a warm, homey feeling to it, with an air of caring and compassion. If I understood correctly the information I had from the social services, my mother's sister had passed away within the last few years.

After introducing myself to the funeral director, I briefly explained why I was in St. John's. "I'm wondering, sir, if you have obituaries dating back to the last two to four years?"

"Yes," he said slowly, reluctantly, "but it's not standard procedure to allow someone access to such private, classified information." But after talking for awhile, he mellowed and admitted he wasn't all that busy. (After all, business wasn't dying to get in that day!)

"Hey, let's go for it!" he exclaimed, now intrigued with the mystery.

What an experience! Hour after hour, we both meticulously combed stacks of obituaries, thumbing through one pile after another. Nothing seemed to match, except for one description. The deceased's name was "Nancy" and the name of the sister was Mary Kelley. Interesting. Could both my mothers possibly have the same first name? I would spend several days trying to find more about Mary Kelley. Eventually though, I discovered this wasn't the person I was seeking.

My search continued, taking me from the funeral home to Vital Statistics to the Confederation Building. An eerie feeling came over me when I walked into the Confederation Building. I knew from my social service papers of many years ago

Confederate Building where all
Newfoundland adoption records are stored.

that this was the building where my sealed and
vaulted records were stored. My file was an insig-
nificant folder in their filing system, but to me it
was everything. Those records knew more about
my origins than I knew about myself, and this was
as close to that information as I had ever been.
Everyone was kind and polite, but cooperation?
Not on your life. The system protects well! Obviously, I would have to keep looking on my own.

I went to the social services building, the
archives building, St. Patrick's Roman Catholic
Church and, finally, to the library. The bus system
in St. John's was very efficient and where I could-
n't ride, I walked. I loved riding the bus. It was a
non-threatening way to enter into the daily lives of
the people, keep warm, see the sights, and get reac-
quainted with the city of my birth. My mind was in
a whirlwind as I rode those buses, but one thought
came over and over: *Thank You, Lord, that it's only
You and me on this trip. I didn't have the*

distraction of constant chatter or need to be con-
cerned for another person. I only had to speak with
my heart and talk to God. He was a great tour
Guide.

The city of St. John's began as all cities in the
New World—down by the water. From there the
people built up and over the hills surrounding the
harbor. The old part of the city was something the
residents took for granted—to me, it was special.
Water Street and Main Street sounded so familiar,
because my hometown of Brownsville, Pennsylvania had those same names. When I rode the bus or
walked those little streets, I felt strangely connected. It seemed as though the clock was turned
back to my childhood, and it was a neat feeling. If
my intuition was even partly correct, this part of
town was a link between my past and the present.

This feeling of being reconnected with the city
of my birth was an emotion I hadn't expected. I
was experiencing my roots. I now realized there
had been a void in my life that, until this moment,
I hadn't known existed. Now my heavenly Father
was simultaneously making me aware of that void,
as well as filling it! A satisfying experience.

Friday morning dawned with new purpose.
Today, I would visit the local Salvation Army.
Before leaving my room, my scripture reading
talked abut truth and mercy going with us through
our days. I visualized two angels, one named
"Truth," the other, "Mercy." Together, the three of
us left the bed and breakfast to experience the day.

I chose to walk that morning—about two miles. Physically, I couldn't see my two angels but, spiritually, I was aware of them on each side of me as, hand in hand, we made our way through the snow.

It was blustery cold, typical for Newfoundland, and I must have looked like a walking snowman by the time I reached the Salvation Army building.

Checking in at the front desk, I was told that the gentleman I needed to see had just arrived back in town but was not expected in his office. It seemed that every question I asked received an answer of "No, I'm sorry." However, I was given some paperwork to complete and told that the major would look at it when he came to his office.

"When will that be?" I asked.

"I don't know," the secretary replied.

I completed the forms—slowly, deliberately and in much detail. After all, I had nowhere else to go. *Now, Lord, what are we to do next? Is this a dead-end? These very efficient secretaries seem to have built an impenetrable wall around the people I need to see and the information I need to get.*

Looking up, my eyes noticed a sign across the hall which read, "Salvation Army Bookstore— Open to the Public." Ah, that's what I'll do—go to the bookstore. Then I can stay in this building a little longer, which will buy some time to think and pray.

I completed the paperwork and returned it to the secretary. Going across the hall and up the stairs, I entered the bookstore. My mind certainly wasn't on the merchandise, as I stood in front of the bookracks praying, *What am I to do next, Lord*? An older gentleman walked to my side and kindly asked, "Ma'am, are you looking for something?"

"Yes, sir, I'm looking for my mother." His surprise was obvious. There were certainly no mothers hiding among the bookcases!

"I'm adopted," I quickly explained, "and I'm here trying to find my birth mother." Briefly, I told him my situation, emphasizing that I had to return to Florida in a few days, and I didn't know what to do next. Bless him! He had two adopted children himself, and he became the link I needed. Hurrying to the phone, he called Peter Graves, the Salvation Army major. Mr. Graves had just arrived home after a week of inspections around the Island and was working on his car.

Taking the phone, I introduced myself and asked his schedule. No, he was not going to the office today. He might go in for a few hours on Saturday, but his office hours would begin Monday morning. He took the sketchy information I had and assured me that if anything should develop, he would contact me. In the meantime, we made an appointment for Monday morning. With this small accomplishment, Mercy, Truth and I walked down the hill to enjoy lunch in the café at St. Clare's Hospital.

As the day progressed, the conviction that I was getting nowhere crystallized in my brain. In spite of my earlier resolve to allow no frustrations, a helpless, hopeless feeling overwhelmed me. Quietly, I reached out to God, not in anger or rebellion, but with the realization that humanly I had exhausted my store of resources, and time was running out. All I could do was simply trust Him, but I admit that I was discouraged that Friday night. Major Graves, my only contact, would not respond until Monday, and I was to leave on Tuesday.

I spent Saturday morning shopping for souvenirs and in the afternoon rode the bus to the house of the "bottle people." They weren't home.

When I returned to the B&B Saturday night, I was greeted with a message, "You had a call earlier this afternoon from a gentleman by the name of Peter Graves. He will be in his office between three and four today and would like you to call him."

My stomach did flip-flops! Hurriedly, I found a phone. "Major Graves, this is Joy Budensiek. I just received your message. Thank you so much for calling."

"Joy, I decided to go to my office today, and I've looked through the files. Yes, I did find where a baby was born on December 30, and I have the name of your mother. By law, I am not permitted to give you both the first and last name."

Panic stricken, I sent a flash message to my heavenly Father. *Oh, God, please don't let me ask for the wrong name. Is the last name called the 'surname' or the 'given name'?* But before I could clear my jumbled thoughts, he continued, "Your mother's last name is O'Brien."*

"Please, Major, spell that for me." Carefully and deliberately, he spelled out each letter, and to me each letter became etched in pure gold.

Hanging up the phone, I fell across the bed and cried tears of relief, joy and thanksgiving. For the first time in my life, I had a name! Not a face yet, but a *name*! *Thank you, God, for working another miracle for me.* (There now, skeptics, who laughed when you heard my story! The God Who loves to give good gifts to His children has given me a last name!)

Later that evening, the "bottle people" called, inviting me to supper Sunday night.

---

* The credibility of the Salvation Army should not be questioned. They do not give confidential information. My story is the exception. The Major was not familiar with everything that had happened to me at the time we talked. To the best of his knowledge, he was following the Newfoundland legal guidelines for the dissemination of information.

15

MY GOD LOVES DRAMA

The steps of a good man (woman) are ordered by the Lord:
and he delighteth in his way
(Psalms 37:23).

Sunday morning dawned crisp and bitterly cold.

Before leaving my room that morning, God and I had a chat. *You and I have been walking this journey of life a long time, God, and You know I always go to church on Sunday mornings. But, Lord, this morning I'm not going to church; You and I have a little research to do.*

By 9:15, I was walking (nothing runs on Sunday mornings, including buses) along the cold, silent streets of St. John's to the Queen Elizabeth Library. I could hardly wait to reach not only the information I would find there, but also the physical warmth. Upon arriving, I was dumbfounded. Oh, no, *I don't believe it!* It was closed! As usual, I hadn't read all the fine print on the notice the day before, and it didn't open until 1:00 that afternoon. It was only 9:30 a.m., and it was icy cold, as only a

January Newfoundland can get. No buses were running and I was blocks from the hotel. *Now what, Lord? I'm in the middle of nowhere, I'm frozen, and I need help!*

Go to the other library. It's also an arts and crafts center. There will be a lobby where you can get in out of the cold.

Several blocks later and with what felt like frozen extremities on my body, I pushed open the doors to the library. It was so warm—*thank You, God.* I saw only the weekend cleaning crew. Watching them work, an idea came to mind. *Janitors have keys, even on Sunday. Maybe he will unlock the door upstairs so I can look at the City Directory.*

"Sir, I'm from Florida, and I'm going home in just a few hours. I'm here trying to find my birth mother. I just found out her name and I need a City Directory. Could you possibly let me in the library to look up her name in the directory?"

"What?" the poor man looked bewildered. "You know the library is closed on Sunday. I could get in a lot of trouble if I did that."

"Yes, sir, I understand all that, but you need to understand my predicament. I'm leaving in just two days, less than forty-eight hours, and just last night I learned my mother's last name. This is probably the name that I've been looking for for many, many years. Please, just this once, will you do what you have to do to let me see that book? It will tell me her address; it will tell me where she works. Please, sir?"

My pleas won out over his better judgment. The two of us walked up the stairs, unlocked the first door, then unlocked the door to the Newfoundland Studies area.

"The book I need is right over there."

"Okay, wait here. I'll get it for you."

O—O'Brien. The list was long, very long. "Sir, there are too many for me to copy by hand. Do you have a copier?"

"Yes, but it will take too long to warm up. I'll take you down the back stairs to the basement, and you can use the machine in the maintenance department."

Dear God and angels, I sure hope You are on duty! You know my husband would flip out if he knew what I was doing. Here I am in a narrow basement stairwell, in a nearly shut-down building, with a total stranger. Joy, you've done a lot of dumb things in your life, I muttered to myself, but I think this is rated near the top. Nobody knows where you are; nobody would know if your body was shipped to Timbuktu! No one would even know that you needed to be looked for if you didn't reappear. Please, dear God, take care of Your little one.

I made my copies and the janitor and I returned upstairs. Tucked inside my coat and next to my heart was the precious paper, the key to unlocking my mystery.

Now retracing my steps of the morning, no more thought was given to the bone-chilling temperatures. Nothing but praise welled up from deep within my spirit. *Oh, God of the universe, You know me so well. I love drama and You've given me a full dose this morning.* I was practically skipping down the sidewalk. I was so happy! *Oh, heavenly Father, this is so neat! Thank You, thank You, thank You! I praise You.*

Now that I had a name, I returned to the funeral home to again search the files. I found nothing. Later, I learned that the dates I had been given were wrong.

That evening was my dinner appointment at the home of the "bottle people." What an interesting scenario. Here we were, complete strangers, trying to sort through the circumstances which had brought our lives together. Ed's parents were visiting from Gander, and everyone was intrigued by the mystery.

"I understand someone found the bottle that we tossed off the ship when we were returning to Ft. Lauderdale from the Bahamas," stated Lorrie.

"Yes, isn't that incredible? Three wine bottles tossed into the Atlantic—two are who-knows-where, and the third bottle brings us together."

"How did you get connected with it?" asked Lorrie.

When I told them about my friend finding the bottle half submerged on a Hobe Sound beach and then our "chance" encounter at church, she slowly and deliberately exclaimed, "Oh, my goodness."

"God brought me here, He really did."

"Oh, yes, we believe you, we believe you," Ed and Lorrie hastened to reply.

Ed's parents had been quietly listening up to this point, but now they entered the conversation. "We've got all these telephone numbers, so let's start calling." Ed's dad started down the list, and we could tell by the conversation whether we had my mama or not. As one after another didn't match up, he crossed them off the "maybe" list.

Now an answering machine clicked on. "I am not able to come to the phone right now, but if you will leave a message, I will return your call when I get home." We noted that every pronoun was singular. I'd always had a gut feeling that my mother had not married, so the personal pronouns fit.

"Joy, I think we've found your mom."

"Yes, I think we have too."

That night when Ed took me home, we drove past 312 Telegraph Road. Maybe, just maybe, behind one of the doors in that apartment building was my mother. Time was running out, however. I was down to my last twenty-four hours. How thankful I was that I had followed my intuition to make my return flight on Tuesday rather than Monday.

Monday morning, I returned to the Salvation Army Headquarters on Adams Street to keep my appointment with Major Peter Graves at 9:00. We didn't waste any time. In his hands was a copy of my records. "Yes, Joy, your mother's name is O'Brien. She worked at Bowring Brothers' many years ago. You were born at 9:12 in the morning, weighing five pounds, twelve ounces. She dedicated you before you were given for adoption."

How these little facts delighted me! Most people have heard this information from their mothers all their lives, but this was news to me.

Major Graves gave me a photocopy of the Salvation Army records. I noticed blanks in various places on the page. *Why the blanks,* I wondered. *Oh! They've used liquid paper over her first name.* (I had taught typing for many years, and I knew how much space M-A-R-Y would take.) Major Graves was so kind and helpful. He talked with me a long time, then prayed, asking God to continue to be with me.

"Joy, do you think you've figured out your mom's name yet?" he asked, as I prepared to leave.

"Yes," I replied, "I think I have." He did not correct me or lead me to believe I was wrong in any way. With his blessing, he sent me on my way.

Mary. *Lord, how unique.* What are the chances of having two mothers named Mary?

Normally, my "bottle friends" would have been teaching school on Monday, but the St. John's school district had appointed this day off because they hadn't used their snow days. God is such a masterful Designer. He knew I would be in St. John's today, and I would need these friends to tote me all over town. Upon arrival at their home, I filled them in on the morning's events. "You know," I said, "I think I have this figured out. I think I know where she works and where she lives."

"What are we going to do about it?" Ed asked.

"I'll tell you what, let's call over to the place where she works, ask a few questions, and find out when the shift changes." The City Directory listed my mother's employer as Canadian Hydro Systems. One short call to the company office told us what we wanted: Mary O'Brien worked there and the shift changed at 2:00.

Ed and I arrived in the parking lot about 1:30, parking in what we hoped was an obscure place. Two'clock. Ladies began coming from the building. *In all probability, I thought, one of these women is my mother, the woman who brought me into this world.* Writing furiously, we scribbled license plate numbers of each car in that parking lot. Then, hurriedly, we drove to the address shown in the City Directory as the home of M. O'Brien.

Impatiently, we waited . . . and waited. An hour or more passed, with cars coming and going. None matched. Wait! A small red car pulled into view—we had seen that car at the factory. Breathlessly, we checked the license plate number and it matched. A short, light-haired lady got out, went around to the trunk, picked up her groceries, and turned toward the apartment building. But not before turning to look at us, questioningly.

"Joy, I think you've just seen your mom."

"Yes, Ed, I think you're right."

"What do you want to do now?"

"I have to go to the bathroom."

"Okay, let's go home. We'll get a bite to eat and come up with a plan."

"Sounds good to me."

What was I supposed to do? My mother had already turned down the opportunity to connect with me. I knew my mother was a lady with much to hide. I didn't know why she felt she had to turn me away before, but I did know that God had worked so many miracles to bring me to this time, this place. I had less than fourteen hours before I flew twenty-five hundred miles back to Florida. I didn't want to damage the life my mother had made for herself, and I truly wanted to be kind and sensitive to her feelings. Should I go to her door and ask for some answers or should I return to Florida in the morning, always regretting that I had not met her?

My policy for living has always been to walk through the doors that God opens and stop at those He closes. Nothing profound, but it's worked for me. God had directed my steps to this point, and until **He** shut the door, I'd keep walking.

I was certain of one thing: if I was meant to reconnect, I wanted to be on hand to do it myself. I could not let anyone else negotiate without me being there.

16

ETCHED ON THE HANDS OF GOD

Behold, I have graven thee upon the palms of my hands;
thy walls are continually before me
(Isaiah 49:16).

A great fear of my family and friends in Florida had been that if things went wrong, I would be devastated and alone. That did not happen. God always goes before to make a way, then puts into our lives the right components. Ed and Lorrie, my "bottle friends," were truly my angels. The more intense the situation, the less time it takes to develop camaraderie. That's the way it was with the three of us. I could trust these people.

Following supper that evening (after earlier having watched whom we thought to be my mother enter her duplex), Ed, Lorrie, and I bundled up and set off for "over the hill." I was going to my mother's house! All the way, my stomach was riding an emotional roller coaster.

"Oh, Lord, we are getting close," I prayed out loud. "You have brought me this far, but if in Your love, mercy and wisdom, You see this isn't what I should be doing, stop this car or do something."

"But, God, please don't hurt my car in the process," Ed adds, turning to look at me in the back seat.

"Oh, that's right, God, please don't hurt Ed's car."

Ed stayed in the parked car while Lorrie and I climbed two flights of stairs to her address, all the while taking very deep breaths of nervousness. Gathering together all my mental fortitude, I knocked on the door. Immediately, a female voice said with a Newfoundland accent, "Hello? Who's there?" Lorrie and I looked at each other, both wondering how to respond. Here I was, after forty-five years, about to face my mother. Should I say, "It's me, Mom, the daughter you've had hiding in a closet for forty-five years?" No, I couldn't say that. I had vowed that I would be sensitive to her feelings.

Seconds passed, but it seemed like an eternity. Clearing our throats and shifting from foot to foot, finally Lorrie stuttered, "We are here working on a family history." Opening the door a tiny crack, the lady first looked at me, questioningly, then Lorrie. What a contrast we were—I'm short and dark-haired; Lorrie, tall and blonde.

"What do you want?"

"Are you Mary O'Brien?" Lorrie asked.

"Yes, my dear, that's my name."

Again, Lorrie and I looked at each other, really not knowing where to go with this. I began to ask the questions.

"Did you have a sister who died not long ago?"

"Yes."

"Have you lived in St. John's a long time?"

"Yes." *She wasn't making this easy.*

"Have you ever heard of the Navy base at Argentia?"

"No!" She said emphatically. *Oh?*

"Did you live here in the '50s?"

"No."

"Did you ever have an American friend who was from Argentia?"

"No." *Okay. I'm going to have to become a little more direct.*

"Did you get a call from the social services a few months ago asking you about an adopted child?"

"No." *Okay, Lord, here goes.*

"Do you know anyone by the name of Sandra Lynn?"

"No. I don't." Now her eyes narrowed and shifted from my face to Lorrie and back again. "Where are you from?"

"Florida," I intentionally replied. The social services contact person had probably told her I was from Florida. If it meant anything to her, she didn't let it show.

Okay. Something wasn't going right here. I'm not sure what my expectations were, but I guess I had never considered confusion. There was not any magic chemistry. Lorrie and I just looked at each other, cleared our throats, and shifted from side to side.

"Thank you for your time. I guess we've made a mistake. Have a nice evening," I stammered.

"There are many Mary O'Briens around you know," she said, closing the door. The visit was over and the door was shut.

Was she? Or wasn't she? Had I just been looking at my mother, or had I looked at another woman who had no clue what I was talking about? The facts seemed to say she was *the* Mary O'Brien, the woman who gave birth to me, but she had denied it. Were my questions meaningless to her?

Walking down the stairs, Lorrie asked, "Is she your mom, Joy?"

"I don't know. I honestly and truly don't know." There was nothing else to say.

Ed and Lorrie left me at my door, we said our good-byes, and they drove off into the night. My feet were heavy climbing the stairs to my room. This was my last night in Newfoundland. The day that had begun with such bright anticipation was now murky confusion. *Lord, I just don't know what's going on.*

Even before I took off my hat, coat, gloves and all the things that go with a Newfoundland winter evening, my eyes fell on my little inspirational calendar on the desk. Turning the page for tomorrow morning's devotional, these were the words which jumped out at me: "And the Lord said, I will not forget you. See, I have engraved you on the palms of My hands" (Isaiah 49:8). The inspirational thought read, "We talk about God's remembering us, as if it were a special effort. But if we could only know how truly we belong to God, it would be different" (Phillips Brooks). *Oh, Lord, what are You saying to me!*

Picking up my Bible, I turned quickly to the scripture reading in its entirety found in Isaiah 49:8,15,16: "In the acceptable time, I have heard thee, and in the day of salvation, have I helped you." *Are you telling me, Lord, that it's not the acceptable time? Okay. I can handle that.* I continued to read: "Can a mother forget her sucking child, that she should not have compassion on the son of her womb? Yea, they may forget you, but I will never forget you. Behold, I have graven thee upon the palms of my hands, and thy walls are continually before Me" (verses 15,16).

Don't forget, Joy, you're Mine. I love you with an everlasting love, and it doesn't depend on your circumstances. Of course you have questions; of course you are perplexed, but it's okay. Regardless of who does or doesn't come into your life, I'm here.

God was so close as He ministered to me that night. No, I still didn't know if I had found my mother, and it seemed that even the scriptures were telling me that it is possible for someone to go through such an experience and yet deny the connection. But my heavenly Father turned what could have been a most painful night into a blanket of warmth and security.

My flight would leave St. John's in the morning.

17

"YOU'VE BROKEN AN INTERNATIONAL LAW"

Wait on the Lord; be of good courage
and he shall strengthen thine heart
wait, I say, on the Lord
(Psalms 27:14).

"Hi, do you live here in Newfoundland?" I asked the only other lady in the waiting area for the flight bound for Halifax.

"Yes, I live in Holyrood and am on my way to see my grandchildren. I can tell by your accent that you're not native."

"No, I'm not." Briefly, I told her that I had come to Newfoundland to find my birth mother.

"So, did you find her?"

"I don't know. I know that sounds strange. I found someone who I really thought was her, but she denied it."

The call was made to board our plane.

During the flight, my emotions were in a whirlwind. Newfoundland had become a very special place, and I was leaving it behind, without knowing my mom. *Did I find her?* The question would not leave me. *Did she turn me away again?* I was restless with my thoughts. The flight to Halifax was short and uneventful.

Upon entering the terminal, I saw the woman with whom I had been conversing on the plane. She was holding a beautiful, white crocheted star. "Here," she said, "I crocheted this star for you during the flight, and I want you to take it with you. Consider it a star of hope. I know you're hurt and confused right now, but never, ever give up hope." And with that blessing, she left me. I stood there clutching the beautiful star of hope, trusting that someday things would indeed come together.

Connections were bad, layovers were crazy, and what should have put me into West Palm Beach early in the evening turned into a 3:00 a.m. arrival. My son, John, was there to meet me. As I told him the week's events, a thought came to me: *If I could just run the license plate tag that I thought was hers, I could easily confirm it.* I wanted to know the truth instead of this confusion.

The afternoon following my return to Hobe Sound, a friend who is a major in our local police department "happened" to be in our church parking lot. "Bill, I've just returned from Newfoundland looking for my mom. I think I found her, but I can't prove it. I have a license plate number. Could you run an international check on it?"

"Sure, I can do that."

Guess what? Mary O'Brien matched the license plate number! Now I was *convinced* I had met my mother face to face.

Confirming my mother's identity happened in the best possible place. Not only was I in the company of friends, but also family. My daughter, Julie, was beside me, and I was glad. God takes care of the smallest details. As a mother watches out for the best welfare of her young, so does the Lord watch over His children and takes potential stones and thorns from their pathway.

Now I could be content to wait years for further developments, if necessary. But for one more thing—I wanted to write Mama a letter. But this letter would take some special thought:

• It could not have a Florida postmark—that would be a dead give-away.

• It could not present my information too obviously—she might look at it in disgust and throw it away without reading it.

• I must not write as though I suspected the truth—it had to be non-threatening.

• This letter could be my first and only chance to tell her I love her and wanted nothing from her.

So with all this in mind, I sat down to pen my thoughts.

Dear Mary,

I need to apologize for interrupting your evening a few weeks ago. I was looking for someone with your same name. You see, I was one of those adopted babies of the '50s. If you should ever run across someone with your same name, please tell her I'm looking for her and that I love her.

Sandra Joy

By signing my name "Sandra Joy," I was bringing my two worlds together. It seemed like a good compromise.

I placed all my thank-you letters to those who had been so much help to me and the letter to Mary O'Brien together in a package and sent it to Ed and Lorrie, for her to mail with Canadian postage. I did not put a return address on the letter to my mother, since I didn't want anything on the outside to indicate it was coming from the United States. I enclosed a five-dollar bill to cover the postage. Signed, sealed, sent.

I was shocked when two weeks later I received a call from the U.S. Post Office informing me that the package had been rejected at the Canadian customs office. That meant my thank-you notes and the letter to my mother were still in Florida, undelivered! Absolutely perplexed, I walked into the post office to see what the problem was. "What in the world did you do to make the Canadian customs reject your package?" a clerk loudly asked. I noticed that several clerks were paying close attention to our conversation.

"I don't know; I have no clue."

"This is yours, isn't it?" She was looking at me as though wondering what sort of illegal activity could possibly be involved.

"Yes. That's the package I mailed about two weeks ago. I honestly have no idea what I did wrong."

Out came the big USA/Canadian Postal Regulations book, and together we tried to figure it out. "You've broken an international law!" she finally exclaimed.

"I did *what*?" I couldn't believe my ears. She had discovered a law forbidding the mailing of American currency to another country. This was a "first" for the post office also. Never before had a package been returned for this reason. So, out came the five-dollar bill, and after paying the postage *again*, my package was sent on its way once more.

I could only think that once again angels were orchestrating the unfolding of my drama. God's perfect timing wouldn't allow the package to arrive in Newfoundland too soon. I learned later that the package arrived at my mother's door near the anniversary of her sister's death three years earlier. It was a time when her heart was softened and made tender and ready for its contents.

~ ~ ~

"Mom, you do know, don't you, that if your mother should ever call you, she won't call you

'Joy' because to her you are 'Sandra Lynn'?" my daughter casually asked during one of our days together. I had never thought of that, but it did make sense. I had to remember that the mother I had lost many years before was no longer a teenager, but a lady in her 60s. The last time she had seen me, I was a baby in her arms—a baby named "Sandra Lynn."

But I had to get on with my life. It might be years before I heard my mother call me Sandra Lynn.

But that was not to be.

18

WONDERS NEVER CEASE

*Commit thy way unto the Lord; trust also in Him;
and He shall bring it to pass
(Psalm 37:5).*

Mary O'Brien received the letter on a Thursday. On Friday, a telephone call from St. John's, Newfoundland, showed on our caller readout.

"Mom, are you busy right now," asked my son, Jim, who was at home. "I think you might want to come home and check out this telephone call."

I couldn't get home fast enough! Hurriedly, I was trying to see if the number matched in the telephone book that I had brought home with me from Newfoundland when the phone rang. The readout again showed a St. John's number.

Taking a long, deep breath, I answered. "Hello?"

"Sandra Lynn, this is your mother."

I screamed! I cried! She screamed! She cried! Heaven and earth stood still, and there was no one but us. Together, we laughed and cried and talked . . . and talked . . . and talked. Two hours we talked.

A page in a book cannot possibly capture the emotions of the moment. After nearly forty-four years, mother and child were embracing each other over wires stretching from Hobe Sound, Florida, to St. John's, Newfoundland.

Over and over again, she referred to me as her "baby." How strange to hear myself called the baby when I had three of my own who were now adults. But the clock had stopped for my mother when she had placed me in the arms of the social worker. In those special two hours, I heard not only how deeply she cared, but also the hurt. It didn't take long for me to feel her pain. The pain within her was so deep that to even get close to the walls she had built for emotional protection took all the courage she could gather. How I thank God for the courage which enabled her to place that phone call! To lift that phone and dial my number would uncover a secret in her life that *no one*—no one but her mother—knew about for over forty years.

~ ~ ~

The year was 1950, and winter had come to Fort Pepperell and with it a new batch of American Air Force personnel. Between Thanksgiving and Christmas, the Christmas lights began to twinkle, sparkling over the blankets of snow. The Christmas spirit was in the air, and it was a time for love, laughter and fun.

"Mary, I want to introduce you to Robert, a friend of mine."

Robert was tall, dark and strikingly handsome in his Air Force uniform, and best of all, he was an *American!* Many Newfoundland girls wanted to date an American. These guys were fun-loving, easy-going, with a certain mystic about them. Robert was all these things and more.

And, besides that, these guys had money. It was nothing for him to toss cash on restaurant tables, and presto, food appeared—*lots* of food. It was fun to eat out in restaurants all across town, but it was also filling up a stomach that never seemed quite full.

Mary felt so special when she was with him. The way he looked at her and the touch of his hands made her feel beautiful. The chemistry was right between them, and they were young. So, hey, loosen up! Why not have a little fun? They could get married, and she would return with him to Ohio when his tour of duty ended.

Certainly Robert and Mary didn't think of themselves as one among many, but, of course, they were. Over 42,000 American men went to Newfoundland single but returned to their hometowns with Newfie wives. These were the recorded legal marriages. Records don't indicate how many babies were conceived during that time, but the number must have been high, very high. Morally upright, hard-working Newfoundland mothers and fathers were faced with the nameless terror that continually gripped their hearts: they did not want their daughters to become pregnant. They would listen as whispers flew from house to house about who was now "in the family way," all the while holding their own breaths. Such a blow to the family name and family pride was to be avoided at all costs. And if "at all costs" meant living behind closed doors for nine months, going to visit an aunt, or finding some way to get rid of the baby—all in secret, of course—then you did what had to be done. And you never ever told *anyone!*

No! Oh, please, no! Panic gripped Mary when she realized the change in her body. Mama's worst nightmare was about to come true. Grief-stricken, she reflected back to the days and nights which led to this awful realization that she was pregnant.

Winter had ended and spring was in the air. The days had been warm and beautiful with fluffy, cotton-like clouds in the gorgeous blue sky. The nights were so romantic, and love was secretly stolen as they were wrapped in each other's arms. Oh, but now! How could she dash her mother's dream of a better life for her daughter? How could she tell her she was going to be a grandma? How could she tell her there would be another mouth to feed?

In the '50s, there weren't any classes offering counsel and possible options; social programs for unwed mothers didn't exist. Abortions, although illegal, were chosen by some of Mary's friends, but she could *never* bring herself to end the life of her baby. Ask the church for help? No way. Asking them for help would mean that the "cat was out of the bag." Then whispers would buzz all over town and disgrace would descend. What on earth could she do?

"No, Mrs. O'Brien," the social worker stated, emphatically, "we will not accept responsibility for your daughter's pregnancy. We have no more social assistance that we can give you; you must find another way to feed this child."

To live at home and raise the baby was not an option either. Maybe she and Robert could get married right away, have the baby, then return to the States and live happily ever after. Tonight, she would tell him that they were going to be a mommy and a daddy.

"Mary, in plain English, are you telling me that you're going to have a baby and I'm the father?"

Silently, Mary nodded her head.

"Mary, you know I can't do anything about this. I'm in the U.S. military, and I'll be going home shortly. I can't marry you. I'm sorry, but this isn't something I had counted on. In no way am I prepared to be a father. The best I can do is give you some money. Here's $200. Will that cover an abortion? I don't know how much things like that cost. Will it cover the baby being born? Do whatever you have to do. I'm sorry, but it's probably best that we don't see each other again." Pecking her on the cheek, he said, "Good-bye and God bless" and without a backward glance, walked out of her life, never to return.

Four months of being in love, of being happy, now her world had fallen apart. Never ever could she return to her innocence of a few months ago. The consequence was growing inside her, and the responsibility was hers alone. What could she do? She already loved this child, but financially there was no way!

Everyone, of course, knew about the Salvation Army's home for unwed mothers just over the hill, but no one wanted to be faced with the need to use it. A girl didn't just go to the home in broad daylight for a "consultation"—she did that when no one was watching. But, thank God, even if she didn't want to go there, at least it was an option. Rumor had it that those people genuinely cared, and they could be trusted. They didn't judge your "trouble" or look down their noses at you. They were known to care for the body, mind and soul.

Mary came to believe the Salvation Army was her only option.

~ ~ ~

"So, Mama . . . is it all right if I call you that? In my mind and heart that's always been your name."

"Of course, my darling. I'd be happy for you to call me that."

"What about my daddy?" I asked the other question which had been on my mind all these years.

"My darling, there's not much to say about him." She didn't sound bitter, just impassive and matter-of-fact.

"As soon as he knew I was pregnant, he was out of my life. His tour of duty in Newfoundland must have kept him here for several months after I told him the news. I'd see him downtown, walking along the streets and talking with other girls, but we never spoke after that. He had told me he was from the Akron, Ohio, area. That's why I was so hurt when the social worker told me you had been brought up in that area."

"*What?* I don't know what you're talking about." I was flabbergasted. I had never been a part of that area, and I certainly hadn't spent my entire childhood there.

"The social worker told me that an American couple had adopted you and taken you to live in Ohio. I thought that was where you're from."

Suddenly, her response when I had stood at her door a few weeks earlier came into focus. When she had asked where I was from, and I said "Florida," I was certain she would then know who I was. Instead, Florida meant absolutely nothing to her. Ohio would have been the only place to give her a clue to my identity. In her mind, fate was cruel to have allowed her child to grow up in the same vicinity as the man who wouldn't give their baby a name. After all, it was she, not the father, who had assumed the responsibility. (I suppose social services must do what they feel they must do, but just this one piece of misleading information had caused more than its share of hurt.)

"What made you call today and not respond the other times?" I needed to know why she had told the social services she wasn't interested in a relationship with her daughter.

"Oh, my darling, you simply have no idea how much fear I have in me. I was happy to hear from Lydia last November. For so long I had wondered what ever happened to my baby girl. In fact, shortly after I gave you away, I tried to find you again. They wouldn't let me. I cried and cried, but circumstances wouldn't let me change my mind. Every night during these last 45 years, I have wondered and prayed for my baby. I was so excited when Lydia called.

"For the first time," she continued, "I knew you were okay. I knew you had a good life, and I knew that I had done the best for you. I was happy for you, but I hurt for myself. It sounded like you had everything in life I dreamed of—a good family, an education, a good life. *Who was I?* And you must always remember, no one knew about you. Too many years have gone by. My mother is dead. Who am I supposed to tell? It's all just too painful, and anyway what good could come from it? My only need was to know you were okay. I was satisfied. You did notice that I gave you a little medical history, didn't you?"

"Yes, Mama, I did and I appreciate it. It seems we have a relatively healthy family. Thanks for a fine set of genes."

"It's not that I don't love you—Lord, no, it's just the opposite. I kept that phone number Lydia gave me in my top dresser drawer, so if anything ever happened I had that number. No, my child, you weren't ever far from my heart and mind, but there were—and still are—mountains of fear separating us. Remember the night you and that other lady came to my door? You were the shorter one, weren't you?"

"Yes."

"I couldn't decide which one you were. Your daddy was tall, just like the other woman. And you looked so much like your grandmother that it scared me. I had company that night, so I couldn't let you in. Remember, no one knew, and for me to invite you in with company sitting there was beyond anything I could do. But when my company left I wanted to call every motel around and see if just maybe you were at one. I was afraid to."

In retrospect, most of our conversation had to do with the past. After all, we had 45 years to talk about. I didn't ask her a lot about her present life, and she didn't offer to talk about it. She did tell me she was about to retire and so happy to do so. Our conversation led me to believe she had never married and siblings have yet to be mentioned. If there are any, I'm certain they have not made any attempts to make contact. For Mary O'Brien to have initiated the call spoke volumes to me. I now knew it was fear that prevented her from responding to me at the earlier opportunities. I could not find fault once I knew the path she had walked, and I was so thankful I had not become bitter during the waiting.

That week, both she and I called each other several times. We needed the reassurances that this hadn't been a dream. There really was flesh and blood—our own, in fact—on the other end of the line. We were both "for real."

19

"I'M SO GLAD YOU CAME"

For I know the thoughts that I think toward you,
saith the Lord, thoughts of peace, and not of evil,
to give you an expected end
(Jeremiah 29:11.)

Time passed, during which we continued to connect by phone. Cards were exchanged, and we tried to celebrate special occasions as much as we could with so many miles between us.

"Mama, I have a great idea. Why don't you come to visit me and meet my family?"

"Oh, no, my darling—no, my darling, I can't do that." I could tell the idea was more than she could handle. "No," she continued, "the doors have been locked too long, the pain is too great."

"Well, then, Mama, what do you think if I come to visit you?"

"Oh, **no**, you can *never ever* do that!"

"Okay, don't worry, Mama. I promise I'll never again just appear on your doorstep; you don't have to be afraid that I'll do that to you."

I had also made the statement that I would never again come to Newfoundland unless she asked me, but over time, I realized she would never ask me. She truly did bear too much pain, and the trauma would be too great for her to ever willingly open the door any wider than she already had. If our relationship ever went beyond the telephone and mail, then I must take the initiative.

Yes, Joy, I began to reason with myself, *you're the one who'll have to do something about this. You don't go looking for trouble, but if it comes your way you deal with it. In all probability your mama is the same way. She won't come looking for you, but it will be okay if you go to her.* Once again, I asked God to open and close doors as I made plans to make another trip to St. John's.

Why not return to Newfoundland in January during the college's intersession, when I could easily be relieved of any teaching responsibilities? I knew Mama had a close friend named Sharon whom she had finally told about me. All I had to do was locate Sharon and ask her to be the connection between my mother and myself. *Yes, Lord, if You'll help me, I think this might work.*

January 17, 2000, arrived, and again I was on a flight taking me to the scary unknown. Yet I was confident that the God Who had begun a good work would complete it. It simply remained to be seen how He wished to do it.

Upon arriving in St. John's, I spent the first night in a very small room which, quite honestly, gave me the creeps. Fortunately, I was so tired that it didn't make much difference, except the room was so cold I couldn't take a shower. Added to that personal problem was the fact that my luggage had been lost along the way. I had no clean clothes, so a shower didn't matter anyway!

The next morning I was tempted to fret. *Lord, I didn't come here to spend all of my time on the bare essentials of life. Please settle these housing and clothing problems quickly so I can get on with important things.* I began to call other lodging places in town, but either the prices were too high or nothing was available.

"Did you have a good night's rest?" the gentleman asked when I went to check out. "Was everything okay?"

"I'm not one to complain, sir, but it was rather cold."

"How long are you going to be in town?"

"I plan to stay another week at least."

"Are you interested in staying in one of our new rooms?"

"Oh, yes, sir. I think that would be a pleasure."

"Book her in with a senior citizen's rate for the week," he instructed the clerk. "If the corner room is empty, put her there."

When I opened the door to the lovely room upstairs, I felt the Lord's presence very close. *Here, Joy, enjoy this little room I've prepared for you. I am still directing your steps.* Once again, I had that feeling of having returned "home."

Thank you, Lord, You are so good to me!

I hoped part of this trip would give me some insight into my ancestry. In the phone conversations with my mother, I had been unable to learn much about my grandparents. Mary's father had never been in her life, and to her he didn't exist. Apparently, he had been killed in the war, and she had only a vague memory of him. He had never been in her life, so why should we bother with him now, she wanted to know! The subject was closed.

On the other hand, my grandmother must have been very special—so special, in fact, my mother didn't want to talk about her either. Again, memories were too painful. So it was extremely difficult to do a genealogy search without names and cooperation.

A couple days were spent looking at genealogical material and revisiting the city, but I was not really accomplishing what I came to do. It was time to step out of my comfort zone, quit procrastinating, and attempt to contact my mother. I was scared.

It was Friday and I had to find Sharon. I knew only her first name, where she worked, and that she was tall and blond. *Okay, God, I need help.*

My plan was to call the factory where Sharon worked, choose a last name at random, then when the receptionist would say they didn't have a Sharon "Jones," hopefully she would continue by saying they did have a Sharon _____. Presto, I would have the name I needed! I didn't expect it to be easy.

I honestly and truly picked a name out of the air, gathered what little courage I had, breathed a prayer, and picked up the phone.

"Do you have a Sharon Parsons who works at your factory?"

"Yes, we do." *What! You don't mean it!*

"Is she tall and blond?" I managed to ask, after the shock of the moment subsided.

"Yes, she is." I nearly dropped the phone!

"Could I please have her address or telephone number?"

"You're not a bill collector, are you?"

"Oh, horrors, no!"

I not only had her name, I had her phone number! *Oh, dear God, this is unreal!*

This was progressing much too fast! And I was getting more and more nervous. Pacing the room, I reasoned with myself. *Now, Joy, get a hold of yourself. God has brought you this far, and He'll help you the rest of the way. Just pick up the phone and do it! Okay, here goes!*

"Is this Sharon?"

"Yes, it is."

"Sharon, do you work at North Atlantic Builders?

"Yes, I do."

"Do you have a friend by the name of Mary?"

"Yes, I do."

"Are you where you can talk?"

"Yes."

"In private?"

"Yes."

"Well, Sharon, this is Mary's daughter, Joy. I am up here from Florida."

There was a sharp intake of air and an emotional, "Oh, my God."

"I promised my mother that I would never again just appear on her doorstep and I won't. But you know what? We will never make connections unless I take the initiative. Will you be our go-between? If you don't think this is a good idea, we won't do it. If you do think it is a good idea, we'll go for it."

"I must talk to Mary about this. I'll call you back this afternoon."

The wait was long, terribly long.

Later, Sharon filled me in on the details of those long hours.

"She *told* me she would *never* be on my doorstep again." Mama was very, very upset.

"She isn't on your doorstep, Mary! You don't *have* to see her if you don't want to. She'll just go home, and you might never meet her. It's your choice."

My mother struggled for two hours before Sharon was able to calm her down. "Okay, Sharon, okay. I guess she really couldn't have done it any differently. I'm going out of town this weekend; we'll just have coffee before I go. If I like her, we'll meet again; if I don't, this is it! Call and tell her that we'll pick her up at the hotel lobby in half an hour."

"Joy, how would you like to go have coffee?" Sharon was inquiring over the phone.

"Absolutely. Is she upset?"

"Well, initially, but things have calmed down, and she's consented to see you. We'll be at the hotel in half an hour to pick you up."

Half an hour seemed like two hours. In that time, I realized I was not reacting as I thought I would or should. Where's the Kleenex? What should be one of the most emotional moments of my life, wasn't. At least, not with tears. Now that I would soon actually meet my mother face to face, I didn't feel all that different. I wondered about that.

As I walked down the steps into the lobby, I saw my mother coming in the door. She was smiling, and I smiled. After hugging each other, we walked outside and got in the car. I didn't experience an adrenaline rush of emotionalism. There was not this big grandiose "once-in-a-lifetime" moment. We were simply a mother and daughter going for a drive together. Our conversation wasn't stilted, but was warm with overtones of camaraderie. The past was history, and we were together again, seeking a new relationship and understanding. We were not only mother and daughter, but also friends. I was glad I had not been crying.

She told me about her previous arrangements to be out of town. "Oh, my darling, if I would have known about this, I would not have agreed to be gone." She seemed sorry it was working out this way. "But I'll be back on Monday."

Later, I learned from Sharon that sometime during that weekend my mother called her friend and expressed her concerns. "This is the most miserable weekend of my life. My daughter's in town, and I'm sure she's freezing to death. There's nobody to fix her any meals. What is she doing all of this time, just roaming the streets and riding the bus? She needs her mama to take care of her."

The maternal instincts had clicked into gear—and it felt great!

20

KINDRED SPIRITS RECONNECTED

*Lord, thou hast been our dwelling place
in all generations
(Psalms 90:1).*

Mama "needed" to be out of town because God had another very special experience for me. I knew that many years ago my mother attended the Salvation Army church at Lighthouse. I wanted to attend a service—to participate in the church of my roots. The last time I was there, I was probably tucked under my mother's heart, still in the womb. What did I expect to find at this church? Well, I visualized old ladies sitting on the front row, cackling out some old tune. I couldn't have been further from the truth.

If someone would like to turn the clock back forty years or more to an "old-time" evangelistic service, the Lighthouse Salvation Army Church is the place to go. They raise their hands in worship and express themselves with "amen" and "praise the Lord." The people truly love to walk with Jesus, and it is obvious in their selection of choruses and hymns, as well as their gusto in singing. Their music is spirited and joyful, sung with the accompaniment of both a traditional band and additional guitars and drums.

~ ~ ~

I have never kept a diary—should have, but just didn't. But for just one day of my life I actually put on paper the emotions of the day. Those pages went like this:

"Reluctantly, as always, my eyes came open to peer out from the comfy pillow where I had had a great night's sleep. The sky was blue, and there was actually sunlight beaming in the window—but not for long. The weather never stays 'put' for more than five minutes in Newfoundland. Today was the day. Today was the day that I would go again to the church of my mother. Some may say that I was a 'new' visitor that I had never been there before—wrong. I had been there before, they just hadn't seen me—not even the little pouch in my mother's tummy. That would have been a dead giveaway, and that was unthinkable.

"But today, over 40 years later, I was going home. No one else seemed to notice how monumental this experience was. They probably whispered among themselves at what this strange lady was doing, coming to their church via taxi, in the dead

of winter, and then of all things crying and crying
and crying. Not convulsive sobs, just that kind of
soft weeping that comes from way down inside,
with no ability to stop.

"I was home. I looked around the building.
Neat, clean and plain—I was comfortable with that.
The people were okay. I especially looked at the
faces of the older women. Did they recognize me?
Did I remind them of someone from long ago?
Would this have been my network of friends had life
permitted me to stay here?

"I saw the stages of my life pass before me in
the program that morning. Children were obviously
important to this church. They received two special
messages, directed to them, and gave their little
voices back to the eager adults in 'Jesus Loves Me.'
This was not all that different from the little church
in Brownsville, Pennsylvania, where I too had
heard the stories of Jesus from people who loved
and cared about me.

"One petite, dark-haired girl seemed to be the
official keyboardist. She looked like a younger ver-
sion of me—she played the piano like I would have.
Her face was young and clean, kissed with innocence, yet bright with life. That was me. The 'me'
who had grown up in a different time and a different place, yet in some strange sort of way, I saw
myself as a teenager growing up in the Lighthouse
Church.

"And then there was the young mother on the
back seat with a beautiful six-month-old baby girl

with fat pudgy cheeks and an attentive husband. They were a beautiful family, just like my family of a few short years ago. Dear God, what a trip back in time.

"Yes, I was just the strange 'visitor' from Florida who took a video of just an ordinary service, but they couldn't see or possibly know. I was much more than that. I was one of their 'babies' who had come full circle this cold morning in January.

"I could have shut my eyes and imagined I was home—either the 'home' church of my youth, or the 'home' church of my adult life. The message was the same; the music was the same. God's ways are past our finding out. His sense of destiny for each of His children tends to the smallest detail. The little orphan child, who only experienced this church from the safety of her mother's womb, returned 46 years later—the circle is complete, and I am trudging back through the snow now.

"It's cold outside, the wind is blowing, but somewhere on the east side of Lighthouse, just before I turned the corner, the sun peeked momentarily through the clouds and smiled at me—I smiled back."

The over-arching threads of my life have been incredible.

~ ~ ~

I had this fear that my mother might not return to town until she knew I was gone. I needn't have worried, for she returned Sunday night and on Monday, we reconnected.

Much has been written about the synchronicity of adoption—all of those intangible things that begin to pop up when families are reunited. It's not uncommon for people to have lived close to each other without the other knowing. Sometimes people vacation in the same places. I found this synchronizing between my mother and myself.

We were in the mall one evening when I happened to glance at her. I was struck with what I saw. We had the same identical posture and way of standing. When Sharon was with us, on more than one occasion, she remarked about our having the same gestures and facial expressions. "Mary," she commented on one occasion, "whether you like it or not, she is your child. I've been sitting here watching the two of you and everything about you mirrors the other."

It's uncanny, but we use the same sentence patterns and we get mixed up in our talking, both of us trying to talk frontwards and backwards at the same time. When I get a new pair of shoes or a new dress, I will say, "Now I am beautiful." I have never heard anyone else use that expression, but one day over the phone, I heard my mother say, "Oh, now I am beautiful." I couldn't believe it! Twenty-five hundred miles apart and she said the very same thing!

From my studies on mid-century Newfoundland, I've learned that times were hard. Employment was hard to find, and those who didn't like government assistance often had no other choice. My mama, however, defied the odds and rose above her circumstances. She found a good job and today has a comfortable living. Her eyes twinkle with life, love and laughter. I'm very proud of my mother.

I found her home to be decorated in the same colors as mine. But the last straw was when I walked into her bedroom and discovered we even use the same deodorant! Psychologists spend lots of time trying to determine if we are a result of heredity or environment. There was a time, from my teaching perspective, that I would have proclaimed loud and clear, "It's environment, definitely environment!" I'm no longer so certain. My experiences of the past few years with all its "coincidences" causes me to wonder.

Our days together passed rapidly and it was nearly time for me to return to Florida. The flight left very early, but this time I didn't need to find my own way to the airport. My mama considered it *her* privilege.

Neither of us are into saying long, tedious good-byes. At the airport, waiting to board the plane, I needed to ask one more question. "Mama, are you happy that I came here this week and that we have actually met?"

"Oh, I'm so glad you came!" she exclaimed, looking me straight in the eye. "And it probably would not have happened any other way." Wow! What a confirmation. We hugged and promised to keep in touch. Sitting on the plane, looking out the window, I knew this time I was going home with the wonderful, warm assurance that my mama and I had truly reconnected.

21

EARTHY INSURANCE SENT FROM HEAVEN

"Count your blessings, name them one by one
Count your blessings, see what God has done."
Chorus from "Count Your Many Blessings"
(My adopted mother's favorite song).

"Hon, get a load of this. Here's something from Metropolitan Life Insurance Company for Mary Comadoll." My adopted mother had been dead for over twelve years. "The insurance company's a little late, don't you think?"

"Wait a minute, Joy. An insurance company? We'd better read that."

We read it carefully. The company was informing their clients about changes to their investment policies, and from all indications my mother had an insurance policy which I had failed to remember. The neat thing about the receipt of this correspondence was to realize how God brings things together in our lives when we least expect it. In this case, I received the letter on my birthday.

I don't like to cook—never have, never will. Cookbooks? Never! Only those meals which were programmed into my brain from the growing-up years get placed on the table—meat, potatoes and gravy. A few months earlier, I had received an e-mail from our daughter who was in Guatemala on a short-term missions trip. She was asking me, of all people, for a pumpkin roll recipe. That forced me to actually, physically take a cookbook in hand.

As I leafed through the long-unused cookbooks, I noticed at the back of one of my mother's cookbooks a list of some personal information— doctor's name, car mileage, car maintenance record, three insurance policy numbers, and an assortment of other information. At the time I didn't give this information another passing thought.

Now I remembered those insurance policy numbers and back to those cookbooks I flew! The numbers matched! I didn't waste any time calling the toll-free information hotline. Yes, the face value of the policy was available with accumulated interest as well. I went to the cedar chest, with its memories, pictures and official documents, which I had not touched for many years. *Ah, here it is!* When I had all of the required information ready to mail, I sent the envelope on its way with a kiss on the stamp and began the wait for my unexpected gift.

Some weeks later, on a Saturday afternoon, I found in our mailbox a very thin envelope postmarked from Metropolitan Life Insurance Company. The envelope was so thin, in fact, that I mentally prepared myself for its, "We regret to inform you that you are not entitled to. . . ." But that isn't what it said. Instead was a check enclosed for over \$4,000—money from my mother who had long since passed away!

I like to think that Mom was nodding her head and smiling at me from heaven that Saturday. She would have been so happy! Forty-five years since our lives became intertwined and over twelve years since we had communicated, God had allowed a unique and practical way for me to receive a surprise gift from her. What else was new? That's the way my mother always was!

The check was placed in a bank account to enable me to write this story, telling anyone who would read it, among other wonderful happenings, about the selfless love of a special couple for an orphaned child.

22

FOUR GENERATIONS RECONNECTED!

*So are my ways higher than your ways, and my
thoughts than your thoughts
(Isaiah 55:9).*

"Julie, I think you have a problem," said the nurse practitioner at the Women's Center. "It appears that your baby is in a breech position. Although your due date is still three weeks away, I think you'd better go next door to the hospital. You need a doctor's opinion."

So that's what's going on, Julie mused. For several days, she had felt something wasn't quite right. But breech birth would be easier to cope with than the other scary possibilities tormenting her mind. My daughter, a registered nurse, was now the patient—not a comfortable feeling. *Oh well*, she thought. *It shouldn't be too bad. I'll go to the hospital, they'll turn the baby, and I'll go home to wait out the last three weeks.*

"Mom, what are you doing? Are you busy right now?" Julie questioned over the phone.

"Oh, babe, just cleaning around the house. Company left this morning, and you know how I like to get everything back in order. Why?" I asked, nonchalantly.

"I went to the Women's Center for my regular checkup, and they tell me the baby's in the wrong position. They want to try to turn it, so I'm at the hospital now."

"Oh, my goodness, are you okay?"

"Yes, but if you're not overly busy, could you bring Bart to the hospital? I came by myself in the van, and he doesn't have a way to get here."

"Of course, babe. No problem. We'll make connections and be there as soon as we can. By the way, what room are you in?"

"A labor room on the third floor."

Oh, wow, what a day can bring forth! Our son, John, and his bride, Ada, were married only four days ago. What a happy, eventful time! My husband and I were so happy as they began their own home. The out-of-town family had stayed until Tuesday morning for an unofficial "family reunion." When I awoke that Wednesday morning, I thought, *This is the first day of the rest of your life.* Life was good. Today was also our twenty-sixth wedding anniversary. This time last year, we were in Europe for our twenty-fifth. Today's anniversary would not be as "spectacular," but that was okay. Jim, my "heart-child"—the one of three with wanderlust in his blood—was home for a change and not roaming around who-knows-where. Life was always more fun when Jim was around, and in just a few weeks, our first grandchild was due to arrive.

And now came this call. Neither Bart nor I needed a second summons. We arrived at the hospital in time to hear the doctor tell Julie that he couldn't turn the baby and that the jagged marks on the computer screen were contractions. In his opinion, he thought it was a good idea to go ahead and take the baby that day.

"When?" Julie asked, glancing at the clock. It read 4:20 p.m.

"You and your husband will be a mommy and a daddy before 6:00."

The stunned about-to-be grandpa soon arrived; and shortly after 6:00 that evening the cycle of life took one more turn—a new generation, Kaitlyn Renee, arrived. What an incredible experience! I remembered the night Julie was born. It was awesome to be in tune with Mother Nature and other mothers the world over.

Katie needed the support of the preemie incubator, so we weren't able to cuddle her that night. But, oh, how we loved her! Everything about this precious little gift of life reflected a creation of God. Her high cheekbones resembled those of the American Indian, which comes from her handsome daddy. Was that a hint of golden hair from her mama? Already, we could see that she had plenty of spunk and, definitely, a good set of lungs. Hopefully, she had some of her granddaddy's genes, then her world would have some orderliness to it. And, much to my delight, I knew in my heart that in this tiny bundle, an eighth of her was Newfie. Believe me, I was right proud of that!

~ ~ ~

Julie and I had often talked about visiting Newfoundland together. I had now been there on two occasions, but no one else in the family had as yet. I began to dream again. Bart and Julie's life would continue to move on and that probably would mean a literal move from Hobe Sound. If she were to go to Newfoundland with me, it would have to happen soon.

Julie and Katie bundled up for a Newfoundland winter's day

Making the trip in January was becoming a habit. Why not? So the plans were made for three generations—Julie, six-months-old Katie, and myself —to connect with the fourth.

There are some things the brain simply cannot fathom without experiencing. One of those "mysteries" is taking a Florida child to Newfoundland in the middle of winter. Julie had never really seen falling snow, much less three, four, five or, some-times, six feet. She asked simple questions like, "Mom, what happens to all of this stuff? Mom, what makes it go away? Where does it all go?" I'd never thought about it. Snow just comes—and goes. After growing up in Pennsylvania, I was used to it. She was not. Poor Florida child never did fig-ure out that you truly did need to "bundle up" to go outside. But the "cold" was only physical.

"Oh, my darling, you're finally here! It's so cold out. It's always cold when you come." Waiting for us just inside the luggage claim area was the wonderful woman who gave me the gift of life. We were surrounded by tourists, but Julie, Katie, and I were *not* ordinary tourists. We were family recon-necting, and our hearts were warmed as we greeted one another.

I like to think that my birth grandmother, Margaret, and my adoptive mother, Mary, have found each other somewhere in heaven. Imagine their conversation and how they must have com-pared notes! Surely they sensed a completion, a reconnected feeling, last January at St. John's International Airport. Smiling from their heavenly perch, they watched in silence as the hugs, kisses, tears, smiles and reunion at Gate 12 unfolded toward a beautiful future.

What a delight it was to be able to share the "Newfoundland experience" with Julie. She met my old friends, those people who helped to bring my mom and me together. And together we made new friends. We rode the city bus around town "just for the fun of it." We ran through the snow to the lighthouse at Cape Spear, nearly frozen but happy. Looking at the lights of St. John's from Cabot Tower at night is an experience one never forgets. We know, because we did it. Visiting the local shops with all the Newfie "flavor" was a tantalizing delight, with a unique fragrance of sights and sounds all its own. In between snowstorms that week, we packed as many miles, people and memories into our lives as we could.

But we three generations had not come just to enjoy Newfoundland. We had come because there were four generations who could celebrate. Four generations who had reconnected. The saga that began so long ago and which had taken so many turns had now come full circle—the bellybutton had been found and RECONNECTED.

23

IRISH DESCENT, MOST DEFINITELY!

May your purse always hold a coin or two.
May the sun always shine on your windowpane.
May a rainbow be certain to follow each rain.
May the hand of a friend always be near you.
May God fill your heart with gladness to cheer you.
An Irish Blessing

Even before I began my search for my birth mother, many times in conversation I would tell people that someday I would find my mother and father but that equally important to me was to find my roots. I had this passion to know from where I came.

"Joy, you have to be Irish," said one of my good friends, Jeanne Schwartz, during one of our conversations.

"Why?"

"Because the Irish have a lot of spunk. They make lemonade out of lemons. If an Irishman gets hit, he doesn't stay down." And from that day on, I *wanted* to be Irish. Those were *my* kind of people!

"What nationality am I?" was one of the first questions I had asked Lydia Arnold, the contact at social services.

"Joy, everyone in Newfoundland has Irish blood somewhere in their veins. With a name like "O'Brien," you are definitely of Irish "stock." Yes! That's exactly what I want to be—*Irish!*

So began a quest for my roots that continues to this day.

I was so eager to learn who I was that it never occurred to me that the rest of the world didn't share my curiosity—but I quickly found that to be true, and most specifically, my mother didn't!

"No, my darling, I don't know much about who we are. You had a lovely grandmother; everyone who knew her loved her. She died ten years ago, and I've still not recovered from her death. She worked so hard, cleaning and scrubbing, trying to make ends meet. Then when she was able to retire and take life a little easier, she died of heart trouble. My mother was absolutely the best. Isn't that all you need to know?"

"Hmm. Well, how about my grandfather? Who was he? What was he like?"

"Him? I don't know who he was. He was never in my life. I was told he went away to war and got killed, I guess. No one really knows."

"Don't you want to know? Doesn't he matter to you?"

"No, my darling. I never had a father, so I didn't miss him. That's just the way it was."

"Well, what was his *name*?"

"I don't know. You know as much about him as I do."

"You're telling me you don't *even* know his name?"

"No, and I don't care if I ever do. Why do you have to know? It doesn't make any difference to you, so why should you care?" By now her voice had become somewhat hostile, and I knew it was time to lay off the subject.

Perhaps it didn't matter to her, but it did to me.

My perspective is obviously different. Finding my mother was only one piece of the puzzle of my life—finding my roots was another. Those who have always known their family take it all for granted, never giving it a passing thought. That was not true in my life! I was curious about everything. As one puzzle piece fit into my life's picture, another unanswered piece would appear.

Naturally, looking at a map of Newfoundland was not intriguing to Mama—she had lived there all her life. And she took for granted the *Downhomer*, the monthly magazine which advertised to be "a little part of Newfoundland and Labrador for people everywhere," but the world it opened up to me was bright and beautiful, and I can hardly wait for my subscription to arrive. Which one of those little villages did my people settle in? Were they fishermen? What were the names of the women who through marriage were joined to my family tree? Was I like any of them? The more I searched for my identity, the more significant and important it became.

Getting information from my mother became a dead-end street. Whatever her reasons, she simply wasn't going to talk. But I believed her when she told me she "would tell me more if I knew, but I just don't know." Period.

But God understood my insatiable curiosity, and He knew how much it meant to me to reconnect with my roots. He engineered another dramatic plan.

~ ~ ~

The large community of people I live among in Hobe Sound, Florida, is a close-knit family of Christians whose love and acceptance I have enjoyed for many years. These people were concerned for me when I went alone to Newfoundland, and they cared about my birth mother's acceptance of me. Consequently when I returned from my first trip, all five hundred or more of them wanted to know what happened. Telling and retelling the story over and over again was becoming tedious, so it was arranged for me to update all those who wanted to listen after a Sunday night church service.

"Joy, I enjoyed your talk tonight." Mr. Fortune, a gentleman perhaps in his 80s, came to me at the conclusion of my talk. "You know, about 10 years ago, I needed a birth certificate. When it arrived, I was surprised to read that my birth mother was from Newfoundland. People from the Boston area adopted me. I've been curious about my birth mother ever since I saw that certificate. I can only assume that she went to Boston from Newfoundland in the early 1900s, gave birth and placed me for adoption because she couldn't support herself and a child. I'm getting on in years, Joy," he continued, "and I'm wondering if you can help me like you've helped yourself?"

"Whoa, that's a very long shot in the dark! I'm so new at this myself that I'm not sure where to begin when there's no more information than that. But, I tell you what, I'll be happy to share with you a delightful magazine called the *Downhomer*. It's published by Newfoundlanders, and it will at least give you a feel for your roots. I'm afraid that's the best I can do for now."

Several months later, while reading the newest edition of the *Downhomer*, I was surprised to see a "Letter to the Editor" written by Mr. Fortune.

"Hon," I squealed. "Look at this! Here's a letter written to the magazine by Mr. Fortune. Remember—the gentleman I talked with in February about his adoption? I hope the best for him."

Later, I learned that a lady in Toronto read Mr. Fortune's letter and responded. She searches genealogies as a hobby and was able to give him significant information about his family history. Needless to say, he was ecstatic—over eighty years old and he discovered his roots. Another Newfie had come home.

In this exchange concerning Mr. Fortune's search, however, I was introduced to this lady, Mrs. Holiday. My story also captivated her and once again, God cared enough to send me the very best. (Hallmark, move over!) Each summer she visits St. John's to conduct onsite research; then, during the winter, she returns to her home in Toronto, where the central Canadian archives is literally "just around the block." Miriam Holiday would become invaluable to me as I continued the search for my roots.

The name of my mama's daddy was John O'Brien. "O'Brien" is definitely Irish, and even though the name can be spelled at least seven different ways, it is a relatively easy name to trace. The O'Briens arrived in North America around the mid-1700s, either from Waterford or Cork County, Ireland. It was customary for ships to leave England, sail to southern Ireland to pick up men and supplies for the long, dangerous journey to the "new found land," where the fish were so abundant one could almost hand-catch them. The O'Briens were poor people, so they welcomed the opportunity to see the New World.

Julie and Katie visiting a typical Newfoundland fishing village

Records indicate that the original O'Brien "tribe" settled near Ireland's Eye, a fishing village on Trinity Bay.

The O'Brien's were devout Catholics, and they felt the sting of persecution from the Protestant/Catholic quarrels which dominated a portion of Newfoundland's history. Hopes for a better economic life always seemed to be somewhere around the corner, but it never seemed to happen. Records show that great-grandfather, Peter O'Brien, joined with fifteen other heads of households in petitioning the government for some type of "government handout lest we die from starvation." Days were hard, families were big, and infant mortality was high. But it was stalwart families like these that dotted the Newfoundland landscape.

Finally, John and Jane O'Brien realized they must do something. Like poor people the world over, it seemed that the lights of the city and the steady employment found there might be the answer to their torn clothes and scant food. They packed what little they had and headed for the city and a better life.

The first significant event of their new life was the birth of twin boys, William Thomas and John Joseph, born soon after the turn of the century. I fondly call John Joseph my "elusive grandpa" since no one currently living seems to know anything about him.

That's the O'Brien family history; now to my Grandma King family.

It was summertime again and Miriam Holiday returned to St. John's where her continued searching would take her to the provincial archives, St. Patrick's Cathedral, various parish archives, and local libraries. Mrs. Holiday, also a member of the Newfoundland Genealogical Society, was in a monthly meeting when she "coincidentally" discovered someone who would become another piece fitting into the puzzle of my life.

"Ladies and gentlemen, we are going to begin our meeting today by going around the table for everyone to tell what names they are researching."

"King," answered Mrs. Holiday.

"King?" questioned Gerald Graham, an executive officer of the organization. "Did I hear you right? You're researching the 'King' name?"

"Yes, that's right, but I can't give you any other details. This is sensitive information and I can't reveal any identities. Why are you interested?"

"My grandmother's name is King, and I have done the research for our family going back to the 13th century up to the early 1900s." What a gold mine to come my way!

When I was in Newfoundland in January 2000, I called Mr. Graham and asked if we could meet. He was delighted!

"We're fourth cousins!" were his first words to greet me. Aside from my mom, he was the first person I met whose blood I shared. I scanned his face, wondering if we looked alike. Fourth cousins are far removed, but without question, our eyes were similar!

Generation by generation, Jerry walked me through the family tree. Talk about feeling connected! The King "tribe" came to the New Land through the influence of one man—Pierre King.

Around 1700, Pierre King came from Guernsey, the largest of the Channel Islands. Tradition tells that he married an American Indian named Sarah, and they bore a family of seven children. From their union the entire family of Kings became known.

Pierre King's religious influence was of the Methodist persuasion. The Channel Islands were profoundly influenced by the revival of John

Wesley, with Adam Clarke (the Methodist historian) actually living on the Islands.

From one island home to another, the Kings were comfortable with the sea and its provisions. This family settled in the area just a bit north of Carbonear. Fishing was their way of life. Harsh, intensely cold winters and never-ending snow only caused these stalwart men and women to pull their clothes a little tighter, ignore the gnawing hunger pains a little longer, square their shoulders, tip their noses in the air and bravely face the future as they had for the past century. But sometimes reality had to be faced. The fishing industry simply wasn't productive, and it was time to look elsewhere. Part of the family looked east, across the bay, and settled in a little community called Flat Rock. Life here was easier. Maybe part of the reason was the close proximity to St. John's, and trips to the city became monthly, rather than yearly affairs.

It was inevitable that part of the family would eventually move into St. John's. Looking through census records, city directories and other archival information, is where I began to connect. These newly arriving ancestors settled close to the center of town, with street addresses such as Signal Hill, Holloway Street, Water Street, and Duckworth Street. Familiar? Yes! These names on paper quickly became memories of streets walked during my visits to St. John's. Over one hundred years later and under circumstances far removed, this was the very section of town to which I found myself drawn. It's in the blood.

~ ~ ~

Why are Englishmen referred to as "genteel"? Why do Germans have such a strong reputation for good workmanship or compartmentalized thinking and structure? Over time these tags were carried through the generations. But why did it happen in the first place? Is there an element of fundamental truth in thinking patterns? Thomas Cahill in his book, *How the Irish Saved Civilization*, stated, "The Irish can't be expected to invent . . . because they can't settle down long enough to get any serious work done." Well, well. Maybe there is a point to be made here, but let's not forget this world is a much happier place because the Irish know how to live and love life!

And as every person has his or her own worldview, is it possible that there is a "national" way of worship—a worship that comes natural? I have noticed that the Irish seem to be more "in tune" with creation. Even their cross has a world superimposed on it, with the idea to show both the redemption of Christ and the recognition of God as the Creator of the world. But not just *the* world—*their* world.

An Irishman has a refreshing, simplistic way of seeing God every day, all day. From the earliest recorded Irish history, we find the mothers praying for their families, all the while stoking their hearths: "Lord, please, as I am preparing warmth for my family today, will You prepare their way. Watch over my little ones." Records show that these simple people didn't mind talking to God about the mundane things of life—after all, He was their friend, their guide. Their concerns were His concerns. Song and rhyme came easily and often to their lips. Their religion was one to be enjoyed. Certainly the basic doctrines of the church rang clear, firm and true, but they had a unique way of knowing how to walk and talk with God.

My fascination with the Irish became more than stuffy old books, for my heart identifies with them. Music for me has always been a profound expression of praise to God. And no wonder, that's the way generations before me have worshipped Him. To split the fine hairs of theology has always been a subject I've had no interest in debating. I know God and He knows me. We walk and talk together. (I am keenly aware that pure doctrine is necessary—it's just not my interest.)

To the Irish soul, the beautiful world God created is very real. The majestic night sky, the bird on wing, the roar of the ocean, or the view from a mountaintop can literally be painful in its beauty. Are those enjoyments of life and beauty characteristic of only the Irish? No, of course not, but this peculiarity does run strongly in our blood.

As a relative newcomer to Irish identity, my world has opened even wider to a sense of creation and redemption. The great God of the universe personally cares about every detail of His creation and He has provided redemption through His Son, Jesus Christ. Through Him, I can walk with a smile on my face, a lilt to my step, and an assurance that He has everything under control.

Life is good. God is good. And I am happy!

REFLECTIONS ON THE JOURNEY

For the next few pages I will indulge
in what most every writer does
who writes on the topic of adoption —
reflect on the journey.
For some reason we feel
we have a thing or two to share.
Since we've been there,
done that, or something similar,
we have this inner need to
help our fellow travelers.
These pages are written from
a laywoman's perspective, with
some suggested do's and don'ts.
Regardless of what side
of the adoption prism you are on,
I sincerely hope you will receive
some insight, encouragement, or
perhaps just reflections on your journey.

BIRTH PARENTS ~
THE GIVERS OF LIFE

Guess what? Without you, adoptees wouldn't be on planet earth—now is that profound or what? *Thank you for giving us the gift of life!* Perhaps some aspects of our lives since birth became twisted along the way, but we are living persons only because you allowed us to live. That's no small fact, since some birth parents were probably tempted to take the easy way out and have abortions, but we are so grateful you did not choose that option.

The following thoughts are written in the first-person vernacular but they are meant to speak for adoptees the world over. While I cannot truthfully speak for every person who is adopted, I am confident that a majority would share these same sentiments.

• I love you. And because I love you, please know that I have no desire to hurt you. No doubt there were those involved in your circumstance of life who did hurt you and I'm sorry that's true, but I'm not one of those. One definition of love is "that which acts in the best interest of the one being loved," and that beautifully expresses my love for you.

• You need to understand that I was not in your particular situation, but by nature, I am curious about all that pertains to my own life. Not only do you know all about yourself, but you also know the complete story of *our* circumstances. On the other hand, *I* do not know *anything*. My motives for wanting to know about myself are not mean-spirited, nor am I being snoopy just to make you uncomfortable. I only want to know who I am. But you must remember that your history is also *my* history.

• There's no need for you to be burdened with guilt, frustration and shame. The majority of adoptees have no desire to make accusations, nor to be upset with their birth parents. Times truly have changed. In the past, things were hush-hush, but, for the most part, that is no longer true. With the resources you had and the societal pressures you were under, I probably would have made the same choices. Don't waste your emotional energy on the "might have beens" or "should have dones." Enjoy today.

• You *do* occupy a special place in my heart, and no one can replace who you have been in my heart and mind over the years. You were the heroine and/or hero of my childhood fantasies. You have kept your youth longer than most others. My mental picture of you is young and beautiful. Never mind that years may have stacked up, you are still the "elusive unknown" prince or princess of my imaginary wonderland.

• However, circumstances have made it possible for me to have not one but two sets of parents. I'm sorry it had to be this way, but that's the way it is, and nothing will change this fact. When adult adoptees seek their birth parents, the majority wish to establish more of a sister/sister (brother/brother) or aunt/niece (uncle/nephew) relationship. This does not make you any less special—it's just what has happened over the years as we have developed our own strategy for dealing with life.

• "Why have you waited so long to begin searching for me?" a birth mother asked her child. The answers include: because I have been living my own life, with its plans, dreams and goals. I grew to be an adult, received an education, married and raised a family. My adoption always occupied part of my thinking, but I simply did not have the time and energy or, in some cases, the finances, to do more than meet the routine demands of life. Statistics show that it is usually in the middle years that adoptees begin to search for their birth parents. Why? First, our own nest has become less crowded and we have more time on our hands. Secondly, the passing years prod us into action. And thirdly, the need to know medical history becomes a higher priority.

• The intensity of a newly reunited birth parent and child will vary from circumstance to circumstance. After the initial emotional high of the search and reunion, reality begins to settle in. Most of the other "parts and pieces" of my life haven't changed. I still have my own family, my job, and all the other activities currently a part of my life. What you might perceive as lack of continued interest or less time spent with you is not intentional. Please remember that there have been two distinctly different paths meandering through life for many years. True, the paths have once again intersected, but it is quite easy to spin off into those "separate" worlds again. I guess we both need to work together to keep our new relationship from being two ships passing in the night.

• In some situations, the load of guilt, remorse and shame you have carried is extremely burdensome. I urge you to seek help. You could be tempted to think, "Why should I bother after all these years?" You owe it to yourself to lay down the solitary load you are carrying. There are support groups available, with wonderful, caring people who are ready and willing to listen and cry with you—yes, even laugh sometimes. I know—I've been there, done that. And I've listened to many birth mothers share their story for the first time, and it was so neat to see other mothers identify with the burdens carried for so many years. Churches and various other ministries are also available to help you find forgiveness and make peace with God, your family and most importantly, yourself.

• The laws regarding adoption are rapidly changing. I urge you to be prepared for the search that one day may reveal a part of your life which you thought to be long buried. With the advent of the Internet, the ability to remain removed from the past is becoming a greater challenge every day. If, against your wishes, you are found, begin to work through your situation, one step at a time, one day at a time. Until recent years, it was easy for adoptions to be shrouded in lies, secrecy and mistrust. It is time for that cycle to be broken, and as painful as it may be, you can be the catalyst to begin the healing process. Sometimes it so happens that when no one supposedly knows anything about your secret past, it comes to the forefront that you are the *only* one who thinks it is a secret.

I began this message, dear birth parent, with an expression of my love, and I want to end the same way. I truly do *not* hold a grudge, but neither am I blind, deaf, or dumb. Yes, without question, my life would have been completely different had you been able or had you chosen to keep me, but that's life. Now let's look toward the future— together. The key word is "together."

ADOPTIVE PARENTS
~ KEEPERS OF LIFE

It's not uncommon for people to ask me, "What did your parents do right? You seem to be okay with your life. What was their secret?" That's a good question, but one that was never much discussed in my family. The thoughts listed below serve two purposes: 1) a tribute to my adoptive parents, and 2) some suggestions to new parents who are enjoying the rewards and challenges of adoption.

• The fact that my adoption was never an issue is significant. Why must adoption be talked about every day? What good does it do to constantly remind a child that he or she was "grafted" into the family tree? What might be considered positive could take some strange turns in the mind of a child, and constantly reminding him of his adoption could have the opposite effect.

• But, on the other hand, to totally ignore the fact could be equally devastating. There will come times in the development of children when their adoption will move to the forefront of their thinking. When this happens, then talk about it, and if necessary talk about it again and again.

• Tell the truth as the need arises. Obviously, you shouldn't tell a four-year-old that his mother was a prostitute or any other details of his story that could be equally disturbing. Children have an amazing resiliency to handle just about any information, but you will forever put yourself in an unhealthy position if you do not begin by telling the truth to whatever degree it should be told at the time. Be in tune with your child at all times. Be sensitive to their moods and questions and be wise in your discernment. Too much, too early, can be just as devastating as too late.

• Allow your child to touch, show, and tell his story. However skimpy and sketchy are the tangible proofs of his "other life," allow access to those things. In retrospect, I think this was one of the biggest blessings my adoptive parents gave to me. I always knew exactly where my "stuff" was and I had unhindered access to it. I could talk about it any time I wished. I could show my friends. I could put on the old 8mm reels of tape which were taken in Newfoundland. Unwittingly, my parents helped me develop a sense of self-worth and even pride in who I was.

• Recognize that someday in all probability your child will want to search for his birth parents. Don't take this as a personal rejection. The motivation for most adoptees is the desire to fit together the pieces of their lives with no thought to replace you. The adopted parents have already earned their right to a special place in the heart of the child. But remember, every child has a right to know who he is and where he has come from, and you need to recognize how very important this is to him.

In fact, go a step further and offer to help. Some of the most frustrated adoptees I have ever met are those who truly love their adoptive parents, but the parents have become offended and have shut the doors to open communication. Consequently, walls are erected, damaging an otherwise healthy relationship. Do not—I repeat, *do not*—close yourself off from your child during this critical time. Be wise. The behind-your-back activities that your child will resort to will not be healthy. Work together as a team. The suspense you will endure isn't worth it. If your relationship was healthy to begin with, your interest and cooperative spirit will only solidify that relationship, and everyone involved will be eternally grateful.

• Siblings. I've been asked if I felt it is easier for an adoption to "bloom" in a home where there are no siblings, especially biological offspring of the adoptive parents. Perhaps. The ball usually, although not entirely, rests in the court of the adoptive parents. Every effort must be made to not show any partiality. It takes only one or two unintended remarks to lodge deeply within the emotional soul of a child. I know many adoptees who feel just as much part of the family as any biological child. But, yes, in reality, if there are biological children, the adoptive parents have more of a challenge—but a do-able challenge!

• The adoption "grafting" process begins at birth. Studies show that most children have the emotional and psychological capability to understand adoption around seven years of age. Ironically, these same studies show that it doesn't seem to be nearly as big an issue as when a child learns *later* in life—especially if he learns through shocking or "accidental" circumstances. Tell them. For most children it's okay to be different, just as long as they know why and how and that they are loved.

• Please remember someone cried the day you rejoiced. I'm confident that most adoptive parents realize this, and I'm not trying to be melodramatic about adoption—but it's true. It isn't necessary to put down the birth parents to win your place in the heart of your child. After all, you *have* the child—a very, very special gift—because of the birth parents' circumstances. Not often, only a few times in my life, I heard my adoptive mother say, "I wish your mama could see this special moment in your life." It sent a message to me that my adoptive mother loved my birth mother, and because she did, I loved my birth mother also.

Relax with the adoption issue and enjoy being a family. I have friends who adopted the most bright-eyed little guy you can imagine. His parents were there when he was born—an open-adoption procedure. They chewed their fingernails to nubs waiting for everything to come together, at times agonizing over the uncertainty of it all. They traveled many hundreds of miles. But everything is legal now, and he cannot be taken from them. This little fellow has it "made in the shade," and he is the center of their world. Every day they are a mutual blessing to each other. Frequently, this mother asks me questions about my own adoption. She and her husband want to do as much "right" as they possibly can. "Keep loving, laughing and living," I tell her. "Don't get so hung up on the do's and don'ts that you forget your natural instincts to give and receive love. Some things come from the heart as well as the head!"

Adoptive parents, you are special people! On behalf of millions of adoptees, our appreciation is beyond words. You will always and forevermore be our *moms* and *dads*! Thanks!

ADOPTEES
~ MY FELLOW TRAVELERS

- Keep in perspective who you are. You may have several last names lined up in your "pedigree," but never forget that your heavenly Father is first and foremost and your self-worth comes from Him.

- Do not carry unnecessary guilt. If you do have a problem with guilt, make every attempt to look objectively at the entire picture of your life. Babies don't ask to be born. Babies don't determine their circumstances. Babies don't make or break adult relationships. *Adults make their choices.* Wishing you had never been born or thinking that you've messed up everyone's life is an exercise of futility. Adult frustration and abuse often cause the child to feel responsible for such attitude or actions. Rubbish! *You* had *nothing* to do with the early circumstances of your life, so do not carry guilt for situations over which you had no control. It's emotional baggage you don't need.

- Do not be afraid of your curiosity. Most everyone in the world can look in the family mirror and see himself or herself. You haven't yet had that privilege, but there may come a time when you will want to look for your birth family. I say, Go for it! There's no guarantee, of course, what your search will reveal, the reactions you'll experience, or the drama and perhaps even the trauma that will come because of your search, but I think most everyone who has taken this step will agree it's worth it. I have found the calls, the knocking on doors, and the writing of letters to be worth all the time and effort they took.

• Your adoption *does* make you *special*. Most of the books written about adoption tend to highlight some of the more negative aspects, and God knows there is a lot of truth in every one of these books. But remember, for every book written from this perspective, there are thousands of adoptees who are perfectly happy and content with life. You just need to keep it all in balance.

• Do not be afraid to talk about your life. For many, many years just to say the word "adoption" was like choking out a four-letter word—a word which evoked shame. The times *have* changed, but even if they hadn't, we have nothing to hide. One of my dear older friends, nearly ninety, called me aside one day and went into detail about this person in our community who was adopted and no one knew. I listened as she talked and talked, not really comprehending what she was getting at. Finally, she asked, "Do you have any idea who I'm talking about?" "No, not really," I replied. "Me," she said, nearly whispering, her eyes quickly filling with tears. No one, not even her husband, knew of her background. It felt *so* good to finally talk with someone about it. For the first time in her life, she identified with another person who understood.

• You need to recognize that your emotions will be different from those who are not adopted. I have many adopted friends and, over the course of growing up and especially in recent years, many of these friends have finally come to the conclusion that part of their emotional turmoil stems from their adoption. These mixed up emotions have played out in a variety of ways—substance abuse, attachment disorders, strained marriages, and a hundred and one other symptoms. I encourage you to aggressively seek help. Sharing the fact that you are adopted shouldn't be an afterthought—an addendum. If you are trying to work through some situations, the fact that you are adopted could have a lot to do with your struggles.

• On the other hand, adoption issues should not be a cop-out for every emotional struggle you may have. Life isn't a bed of roses for any-one—every human being has challenges through which they must work. Our lives will be as barren as a desert if we don't have the thorns and thistles which cause our character to blossom into a thing of beauty. It is true that adoption affects us at some of our deepest levels, but it shouldn't be an excuse for every "hang-up" we have.

• I cannot encourage you enough to join an adoption support group. Our local chapter began about two years ago. Wow, what an experience!

Obviously, our only commonality is that each of us is somewhere on the adoption triad, and this helps us gain perspective. Adoptees who listen to the anguished cries of the birth mothers who relinquished their children for adoption many years ago better understand the circumstances, the heartache, and the frustration these women have carried for so long. Birth parents hear the adoptees tell of their needs. In an unconfrontational way, the birth parents hear others talk about what they need and want from a reunion. Issues such as reunion, the need for space, and the emotional turmoils from *every* perspective tumble out. We are no longer "an island unto ourselves," and we begin to look at the entire situation through the prism of the other people involved.

Maybe you don't feel you need this support—and maybe you don't. But you can be an encouragement and blessing to the others. So go ahead, join—you'll be glad you did! Your journey will be enriched by the strong, beautiful people with whom you'll be walking.

• Depending on where you are in life, your family may or may not appreciate your adoption story. Hopefully, your search and the attention that will be given to it will have your family's approval, but don't expect them to be as preoccupied with it as you are. Let's face it, they simply cannot *feel* as emotionally involved in your search as you do. Give your family of today time and space to deal with your identity search without regarding them as unfeeling or uncaring. (That's why a support group is so important—they are people who have the emotional tools to understand.)

- If your adoptive parents are still alive and active in your life, you will face the challenge of conveying to them that there is room in your heart for both sets of parents. While the desire to search for biological parents is normal, you will need the time, patience, and love to convince your adoptive parents that they will *always* have their own special place in your heart. Your actions should not make them feel threatened, but rather a journey to be traveled together. The ball is in your court, my fellow adoptee. To a large extent, you will set the stage. Believe me, the production can be beautiful!

ADOPTEES ARE SPECIAL "SOMEBODIES"!

Obviously, any author who writes on adoption comes at the subject from his or her own perspective. As I mentioned in the Preface, our stories are as varied as the snowflakes. My "being" on planet earth was not the result of a random act of passion; I didn't just happen. God was not taken by surprise when, lo and behold, Mary, my Mama, found herself pregnant. I was not a pesky mass of fetal tissue which, given the circumstances, would have been better off killed and forgotten.

"Illegitimate" and a whole lot of other street names pretty well sum up who I am. But those names come from the world around me and names change. Today it is much more socially acceptable not to have or know your father. One third of all births in America today are not in homes where the income tax returns are filled out as "Married." But even with the social acceptance of today, people just KNOW and TALK. For some strange reason the actions of the parents are "taken out" on the child. This is no small issue. Down through time, these illegitimate children have struggled for identity and acceptance—sometimes on a big scale, sometimes smaller. No matter, the fact remains, we are who we are.

Did you know that the Smithsonian Institution stands in Washington, D.C., today as a mute symbol to one man's private fight against the hurts he received simply because of his illegitimacy? By the laws of eighteenth-century England, James Macie was denied his rights of ordinary citizenship. In later years after a successful scientific career, he was also denied knighthood even though he was as successful as his colleagues. In 1829 he died a wealthy man and sought revenge on England by leaving his entire fortune to America—a country he had never even visited. The name, which he adopted in later in life, was Smithson, and today we have the Smithsonian Institution. Macie is only one example.

But no matter what everyone else thinks, how do I view *myself*? Am I a second-class person? Do I need to internally wear my stigma close to the inner core of my being? Does my illegitimacy provide a convenient excuse for any negative aspects of my daily living, my attitude? Should the circumstances of my birth permanently affect my self-worth? NO! a million times NO! Whatever our circumstances, naked came we into this world and naked we will return—no different from anyone else. Our unfortunate circumstances may have "clicked in" shortly after conception (lack of physical or emotional attention), but that has nothing to do with our worth as a person. Not unlike those born into royalty, we *are* a "somebody"—we have value.

And the interesting thing is that in God's great economy, we evidently have a special place. No one (in their right mind) claims to understand all the ways of God—but here's one to think about.

The year was 1988. Our local church had started a ministry called *Touching Lives for Christ*—TLC. That first year had been an incredible success. Beginning from nothing but an idea, we had, in just a few short months, put a program in place which linked together over 100 young people and sponsors and sent them to ten different mission fields for a three-week mission trip. Many people worked together to make this happen, but it was no secret, I was the catalyst that God had chosen to make it all happen. What an incredible experience!

That first year was so successful, in fact, that I was inclined to think it couldn't get any better—to do it again would be a let-down and I wasn't interested. I thought we should leave well enough alone and just enjoy the success of last year. However, Hobe Sound Bible Church assumed TLC would continue under my leadership. The recruiting and fund-raising for the second year was to begin in January, but December found me arguing with God. *God, I really don't want to do this. You know how young I am. You know that in my peer group I have always been the CHILD. You know that I have always been the smallest, weakest, tagalong type in my peer group. Why are you putting this responsibility on me again? It's not fair of You to do this to me.* On and on went my monologue with God. I desperately wanted Him to see my side of it.

I will never forget the morning when my silent cries had risen to fever pitch, that I picked up my Bible for my regular morning devotions. I was to begin reading in Jeremiah. To be honest, I didn't expect much—to me those Old Testament prophetic books can get rather long and tedious. The first three verses began as I expected, but verse four caught my attention: "Then the word of the LORD came unto me saying . . ." *Well, Lord, are you going to give me something I can apply to the struggle I'm going through?* With anticipation, I continued reading: "Before I formed thee in the belly I knew thee; and before thou camest forth out of the womb I sanctified thee, and I ordained thee a prophet unto the nations. Then said I, Ah, Lord God! behold, I cannot speak; for I am a child. But the Lord said unto me, Say not, I am a child; for thou shalt go to all that I shall send thee, and whatsoever I command thee thou shalt speak. Be not afraid of their faces; for I am with thee to deliver thee, saith the Lord" (vs. 5-8).

I nearly dropped over. God had just spoken to me. He had used the exact terminology that I had used—CHILD. He had referred to the exact same thing I was struggling with—touching the world with His message. God had spoken, HE would be with me, and make everything happen, in His time and in His way. What an incredible message.

God not only spoke to me that morning on a ministry level, but also personally. No one knows me better than the One Who created me. He knew in whose belly I was formed and the circumstances of my less-than-desirable conception. But the great God of the universe cared enough to not only tolerate me, but to give me a place of service in His kingdom. Talk about self-worth! The circumstances of our lives have no bearing on our intrinsic worth. It is a beautiful gift from God.

And to you theologians, can you add anything to my simple theology, that God delights in bringing beauty from ashes? good from bad? blessings from curses?

GOD SETTETH THE SOLITARY IN FAMILIES

(Psalms 68:6)

It's Sunday. Someday life will bring changes to our family structure, but for right now we enjoy being together on the family pew for Sunday morning worship. Our family includes the original five, a son-in-law, a daughter-in-law, and a grandbaby. We take up nearly a whole pew, but that's okay.

About 11:55 we tend to get squirmy. It's time to go home to a traditional Sunday dinner—roast beef, mashed potatoes, gravy, vegetables, a fruit salad, rolls (store bought), iced tea and dessert. The menu varies only slightly from Sunday to Sunday—there's comfort in the familiar things of life. Sunday is always a special day, and we find solidity in the habits of Sunday.

Around our table you'll meet Jim, our youngest son. Jim is special. He too marches to a different drumbeat. Before his twentieth birthday he had driven all the way from Florida to Alaska. Jim always smiles as he proudly reflects on his adventures, for he never talks about his dreams unless he's certain he can make them come true—he "walks the talk." Today, he is updating us on his career as a pilot and aerial photographer. With a private and instrument pilot's license already earned, he is currently working toward his commercial license. With that license, he can earn a living high above the mundane! Across the table you'll meet John and Ada. John, our firstborn son, married Ada Duren last summer. They live just a few streets away, but often bounce in "just to check on you" or visit John's yellow cat that wouldn't leave home when John did. Weekdays will find Ada at her secretarial job, while John lives his lifelong dream of being a Martin County (Florida) Sheriff's Detective. They are active in our local church.

Bart and Julie are sitting at the other end; they need more room for the highchair between them. First Julie brought Bart into our family, and then on June 7, 2000—our wedding anniversary—they gave us our first grandchild. Bart and Julie are looking toward full-time missionary work, but in the meantime Bart is a roofer while Julie works two nights a week as a registered nurse.

Katie has brought such a special dimension into our life. From the very first moment she arrived—three weeks early—there was a twinkle in her eye and a smile that just won't quit—even at midnight! Her little sister is due to arrive in October.

Seated at the head of the table is "Dad." He's our mainstay—the guy who makes the dreams happen and keeps track of the details. We make a good pair. My dumb adventuresome spirit gets us places he never would have chosen to go, but when everything is said and done, he's usually glad he did. His intelligent, steady, practical way of living gets us back home. (I'm eternally grateful!) For 26 years, we've enjoyed the "adventure" of life together.

A few years ago, we were visiting his parents in Jalapa, Guatemala. Outside their village was a big, beautiful mountain, and I began to pester everyone, "Let's climb that mountain! Come on! We can do it—I know we can. Let's go! What day can we go?" I didn't let up until early one morning we began our trek. Hours went by and the path had long since disappeared. It was a very *high* mountain, and we had already come a long way. My initial excitement had now turned to exhausted exclamations. "*Who* ever had the bright idea of trying to do this! They must have been crazy! I'm tired and more than ready to give up *now*!" I was the dumb bunny who had gotten us into the mess, but halfway through, I was done. True to the sterling nature of my husband, he removed his belt, fastened it to me, and pulled me the rest of the way up the mountain. He's fantastic!

Visitors and family sometimes come to Sunday dinner. The extended family of cousins and friends make life rich and enjoyable. We've lived in our southern Florida community for nearly twenty-five years. We've done a lot of livin' together. It's been a rich journey.

And what about the future?

Adoption stories never end. Good, bad or indifferent, there is always an ongoing sense of reconnecting—or at least, trying to. Both my mother and I are so glad that we have found each other. However, we respect the lives each other had before we reconnected and do not crowd into the other's space. We send occasional letters, make phone calls, exchange gifts and celebrate (across the miles) major life events. We are "comfortably reconnected."

My search is not finished. Somewhere I have a Daddy. I've done a little searching, but it takes time, money and energy. In the fullness of time God will nudge me, and we'll walk into the "unknowns" once again. In the meantime, "Daddy, I wish you well, and somehow I feel in my heart that you aren't too far away—whether just in spirit and soul, or maybe in the next town, I'm not sure. I've changed names and dates to protect my mother's privacy, but the story remains the same. If you should happen to recognize yourself please call, write, or e-mail. I would love to hear from you."

And there is always that possibility of siblings. I'm fairly certain there are some, and I've rather half-heartedly tried to do some research. Someday, that will turn into a high priority. Wow, will that ever be exciting!

~ ~ ~

In this book I've talked about "roots" and being connected—about finding my bellybutton. But what would life be with only the "roots"—the parents, be they birth parents, adopted parents, or both? I thank God for the stems and branches and leaves that also make up the family tree. How incredibly blessed I have been with multiple "roots," and "branches" that I have been privileged to share life with, and to be able to see the "leaves" of future generations appearing! What a sense of belonging!

LORD, thou has been our dwelling place in
all generations.
Before the mountains were brought forth,
Or even thou hadst formed the earth and the world,
Even from everlasting to everlasting, thou art God.
So teach us to number our days,
That we may apply our hearts unto wisdom,
And let the beauty of the Lord our God be upon us:
And establish thou the work of our hands upon us;
Yea, the work of our hands establish thou it.

(Psalm 90:1,2,12,17)

Regrets? Not one.

Celebrating Life

Weddings
(John and Ada)

Accomplishments (Jim)

Holidays
(Bart, Julie and Katie)

Birthdays
(John and Joy)

Daily joy of living
(Grandpa, Grandma and Katie)

NOTES

Preface

Pertman, Adam. *Adoption Nation* (New York: Basic Books, 2000), 259.

Chapter 2

Crdoulis, John. *A Friendly Invasion II* (St John's, Newfoundland: Creative Publishers, 1993), 221.

Chapter 3

Gariepy, Henry. *General of God's Army* (Wheaton, Illinois: Victor Books, 1993), 368.
Moyles, R.G. *The Salvation Army in Newfoundland* (Canada: 1997), 231.

Chapter 8

Lillenas Publishing Company. *Sing to the Lor*d (Kansas City, Missouri: 1993) 800.

Chapter 10

Devotional Calendar. *Footprints in the Sands of Time*

Chapter 11

Devotional Calendar.

Chapter 12

The New American Webster Handy College Dictionary, Third Edition. New York: 1995) 796.

Chapter 16

Devotional Calendar

Chapter 20

Stiffler, LaVonne. *Synchronicity and Reunion* (Hobe Sound, Florida: French Publishing, 1992) 189.

Chapter 22

Cahill, Thomas. *How the Irish Saved Civilization* (New York: Doubleday, 1995) 246.
DeWall, Esther. *Celtic Light* (London, Fount, 1991) 148.
Downhomer Magazine. (St. John's Newfoundland).

God's Special Somebodies

Harvey, Paul. *The Rest of the Story* (New York: Morrow and Company, 1983), 265.

ABOUT THE AUTHOR

Joy has been happily married for 27 years to John Budensiek and is the mother of three children, Julie, John Jr. and James. Bart Thompson and Ada Duren have joined our family through marriages to Julie and John Jr. Grandparenting is the newest blessing with the arrival of Katie Renee and Janessa Nicole.

Joy graduated from Brownsville Area High School in 1971. She obtained an A.A. in Business from Penn Commercial Business College; a B.S. in Education from Hobe Sound Bible College; and a Masters in Ministry from Moody Graduate School.

Joy has taught at Hobe Sound Bible College and Academy for the past 25 years. She was co-founder of Touching Lives for Christ summer missionary ministry of Hobe Sound Bible Church, and full time director for three years. She has personally taken teams to minister in Guatemala, Ghana, Bolivia, Peru, Bahamas, Haiti and Honduras.

She is currently working with the Martin County School District in the Adult Education Program at Indiantown, Florida.

For more adoptee information, I highly recommend Sherrie's book:

TWENTY THINGS ADOPTED KIDS WISH THEIR ADOPTIVE PARENTS KNEW
(DELL, 1999)

The voices of adopted children are poignant, questioning, and they tell a familiar story of loss, fear, and hope. This extraordinary book, written by a woman who was adopted herself, gives voice to children's unspoken concerns, and shows adoptive parents how to free their kids from feelings of fear, abandonment, and shame. With warmth and candor, Sherrie Eldridge reveals the twenty complex emotional issues you must understand to nurture the child you love. This book is also invaluable for adults who were adopted as children. Available at secular bookstores and through amazon.com.

Sherrie has also written four biblically based workbooks for those that have been touched by adoption:

> *Under His Wings...Creating a Safe Place for Adoptees to*
> *Talk about Adoption*
> *Beauty for Ashes...A Healing Path for the Adoption Triad*
> *Twelve Steps for Teens!*
> *Twenty Things Adopted Kids Wish Their Adoptive Parents*
> *Knew—A Study Guide*

All workbooks are $15.00 plus $3.98 shipping and handling
Order from:
Jewel Among Jewels Adoption Network, Inc.
P.O. Box 502065
Indianapolis, IN 46250
Online: www.adoptionjewels.org

AN IRISH BLESSING

"May the road rise up to meet you,
May the wind be always at your back,
May the sun shine warm upon your face,
The rains fall soft upon your fields,
And, until we meet again,
May God hold you in the palm of His hand."

Additional books may be ordered directly from:
Mrs. Joy Budensiek
P.O. Box 8215
Hobe Sound, FL 33475
Online: joybudensiek @aol.com

US $10.95, Canada $12.95
$2.00 shipping and handling